Also by Albert Grandolini in the Asia@War series: *The Easter Offensive – Vietnam 1972. Volume 1: Invasion across the DMZ*

Published in 2015 by:
Helion & Company Limited
26 Willow Road
Solihull
West Midlands
B91 1UE
England
Tel. 0121 705 3393
Fax 0121 711 4075
email: info@helion.co.uk
website: www.helion.co.uk
Twitter: @helionbooks
Visit our blog http://blog.helion.co.uk/

Text © Albert Grandolini 2015
Photographs © as individually credited
Color profiles © Tom Cooper 2015
Maps © Helion & Company Limited. Drawn by George Anderson

Designed & typeset by Farr out Publications, Wokingham, Berkshire
Cover design by Farr out Publications, Wokingham, Berkshire
Printed by Henry Ling Limited, Dorchester, Dorset

ISBN 978-1-910294-08-6

British Library Cataloguing-in-PublicationData
A catalogue record for this book is available from the British Library

Cover: These T-54Bs were destroyed by the ARVN 8th Regiment on the northern sector of An Loc. The men painted their regimental number on the hulls in order to claim the kills and earn 50,000 piaster, around $50, for each tank destroyed. (US Army); VNAF A-1H, serial 135281, of the 514th Fighter Squadron from the 23rd Tactical Wing of Bien Hoa AB – May 1972. It was armed with Mk-82 HE bombs and CBU-25 dispensers (color profile).

CONTENTS

Note: In order to simplify the use of this book, all names, locations and geographic designations are as provided in *The Times World Atlas*, or other traditionally accepted major sources of reference, as of the time of described events.

Abbreviations

AA	Anti-aircraft
AAA	Anti-Aircraft Artillery
ACS	Armored Cavalry Squadron
AFB	Air Force Base (used for US Air Force bases)
APC	Armored Personnel Carrier
ARVN	Army of the Republic of Vietnam, the South Vietnamese Army
ATGM	Anti-tank guided missile
Brig Gen	Brigadier General (military commissioned officer rank)
Capt	Captain (military commissioned officer rank)
CBU	Cluster bomb unit
CIA	Central Intelligence Agency (USA)
C-in-C	Chief-in-Command
CO	Commanding Officer
Col	Colonel (military commissioned officer rank)
Col Gen	Colonel General (top military commissioned officer rank)
COSVN	Central Office for South Vietnam
DCAT	Division Combat Assistance Team
DMZ	Demilitarized Zone, separating North from South Vietnam
FAC	Forward Air Controller, usually airborne controller in observation aircraft
FSB	Fire Support Base
Gen	General (military commissioned officer rank)
GP	General-purpose (bomb)
HQ	Headquarters
KIA	Killed in action
Km	Kilometer
Lt	Lieutenant (military commissioned officer rank)

Lt Col	Lieutenant Colonel (military commissioned officer rank)
1st Lt	First Lieutenant (military commissioned officer rank)
2nd Lt	Second Lieutenant (lowest military commissioned officer rank)
Maj	Major (military commissioned officer rank)
MANPADS	Man-portable air defense system(s) – light surface-to-air missile system that can be carried and deployed in combat by a single soldier
MBT	Main Battle Tank
MIA	Missing in action
MR	Military Region
NCO	Non-commissioned officer
PAVN	People's Army of Vietnam, the North Vietnamese Army
PoW	Prisoner of War
RAC	Regional Assistance Command
RF/PF	Regional Forces/People's Forces from the ARVN
SA-2 Guideline	ASCC codename for S-75 Dvina, Soviet SAM system
SA-7 Grail	ASCC codename for 9K32 Strela-2, Soviet MANPADS
SAM	Surface-to-air missile
UHF	Ultra High Frequency
USAF	United States Air Force
USMC	United States Marine Corps
USN	United States Navy
VNAF	Vietnamese Air Force, Air Force of South Vietnam
VNMC	Vietnamese Marine Corps
WIA	Wounded in Action

CHAPTER 1
BACKGROUND

On 30 March 1972 the South Vietnamese positions along the Demilitarized Zone (DMZ) – that separated North Vietnam from the South – were suddenly shelled by hundreds of heavy guns and multiple rocket launchers (MRL). Shell-shocked soldiers in a series of outposts along the former 'McNamara Line' scrambled out of their bunkers only to be then met by the accompanying onslaught of the regular North Vietnamese divisions – supported by hundreds of tanks that smashed through their defensive lines. Thus began one of the fiercest campaigns of the Vietnam War, but also one of the less well-documented, as most American ground troops had been withdrawn following the introduction of the 'Vietnamization' policy which aimed to hand the South Vietnamese greater war-effort responsibilities. The nature of the war itself at this point had changed dramatically – evolving from a guerrilla one into a conventional conflict that set the trend until the fall of Saigon three years later. The North Vietnamese would learn the hard way how to conduct mechanized operations against a far better organized southern force (the previous volume in this series *The Easter Offensive – Invasion across the DMZ* looks

in great detail at the context of the fighting, along with the growth of both armies: The South Vietnamese Republic of Vietnam (ARVN) and the People Army of Vietnam (PAVN) in the North).

The campaign pitted two sides that had both been significantly modernized and expanded, with the South Vietnamese – aided by America – between 1969–1972 increasing the size of its military forces from 825,000 to over one million – with 120 infantry battalions in 11 divisions, supported by 58 artillery battalions, 19 armored cavalry regiments, and many engineer and new tank squadrons. After years of neglect, Washington also gave top priority to equipping the ARVN with over one million M16 rifles being delivered, as well as 12,000 M60 machine guns; 40,000 M79 grenade launchers, 790 4.2inch (107mm) mortars, 10,000 radios and 20,000 trucks. In addition, to confront the North Vietnamese T-54s, around 56 M48 medium tanks were also delivered by 1972.

By now, the regular force made up less than half of the South Vietnamese forces (535,000 men) being complemented by Territorial Forces which played a key role in the pacification program. They

Lieutenant General William Westmoreland, Commander of the MACV, and Lieutenant General Cao Van Vien, Chief of the South Vietnamese Joint General Staff, sitting side by side. The much politicized ARVN turned the JGS into a mere advisory, rather than an operational, command. The most crucial military decisions remained in the hands of President Nguyen Van Thieu and his four Corps commanders. (US Army)

Different to the US–South Vietnamese dual command structure, the North Vietnamese High Command was centralized around the Communist Party Political Bureau. One of its leading figures was Senior General Vo Nguyen Giap, Commander-in-Chief of the PAVN since its creation. He also held the post of Defense Minister and President of the powerful Central Military Commission. He is seen here, second from left in civilian clothes, during a 1971 visit to the Soviet Army Malinowski Armored Academy of Moscow, where many North Vietnamese officers attended courses. (Albert Grandolini Collection)

included 282,000 Regional Forces (RF), organized into battalions and assigned to military provincial control, and 243,000 Popular Forces (PF) organized into platoons and assigned at district level. These RF/PF soldiers were now also re-equipped with modern M16 rifles and M79 grenade launchers, but their main task was only to deal with local Viet Cong because, when facing regular PAVN units, they were usually not up to the challenge. Finally, there were more than 500,000 within the People's Self-Defense Forces (PSDF) but these militias were only part-time guards operating at village and hamlet levels, and armed with Second World War M1 rifles and carbines. Tactically, the divisions were grouped within four Corps and each Corps was in turn assigned to a particular Military Region (MR). The 1st Corps operated in MR I which covered the northern part of the country, from the North Vietnamese border to south of Da Nang; the 2nd Corps was assigned to the MR II, covering the Central Highlands and the coastal area between Qui Nhon to Phan Rang; the 3rd Corps operated within the MR III, covering the area around Saigon; and finally, the 4th Corps served in MR IV, containing most of the Mekong Delta Area.

The Military Assistance Command Vietnam (MACV), which was set up as an advisory body to the ARVN, became increasingly less influential with the arrival of US ground units. However, as the war progressed the importance of the MACV advisory assets grew again and advisory structure very closely paralleled that of Vietnamese military command and control organization – with the headquarters providing the advisory function to the ARVN JGS. Under this, a Regional Assistance Command (RAC) was assigned to each of the four ARVN Corps-Military Regions, and under the US RAC Commander (usually a Major General) were two types of advisory teams – province advisory teams and division advisory teams. Each province was headed by a South Vietnamese colonel, and his American counterpart was the province senior advisor who controlled the District and Territorial Forces advisory teams. The province team was responsible for advising the province chief in both civil and military aspects of the ongoing pacification and development programs. In addition to province advisory teams, there was a Division Combat Assistance Team (DCAT) deployed to each South Vietnamese infantry division. Elite units, such as the Airborne Rangers and Marines, were generally organized along the same lines as regular ARVN units, but as American forces began withdrawing from the country, the number of advisors also dwindled. Thus, they now only operated at divisional

and regimental levels apart from in the Marine Division where they continued at battalion level. By January 1972 there were only 5,416 American advisors in the whole of South Vietnam.

In North Vietnam, since the failure of the Tet Offensive in 1968, the main PAVN units had also evolved into a modern mechanized force and were themselves now being greatly supported, but by the Soviet Union and China – who had both delivered heavy artillery and tanks between 1970–1971. However, the motorization phase did not run smoothly because many North Vietnamese divisions could not be upgraded and trained on schedule as they were already deployed in the field, and the PAVN then found it difficult to create units ready for the new form of mechanized and combined arms operations. Mobile training teams were thus sending units forward whilst other regiments or divisions rotated back into North Vietnam for refitting. Yet, despite all these difficulties, the PAVN modernization process continued unabated and led to a force of some 16 divisions and four armored regiments by early 1972. This force of 433,000 men and 655 tanks was also supplemented by around two million men and women, including 870,000 light infantry, which belonged to the Militia Command. Also, some 104,000 'regulars' and 26,000 guerrillas officially belonged to the Viet Cong, who were officially independent from the Central Office for South Vietnam (COSVN), the military wing of the National Liberation Front (NLF) – a fictitious designation allocated to the Viet Cong for propaganda purposes. Within the Viet Cong itself though, morale was faltering and Hanoi was forced to bolster its ranks whilst the COSVN had become nothing but a Forward Command Post of the PAVN that needed constant support from the B-2 Front. However, the PAVN expansion process continued throughout the Easter Offensive despite huge losses and the number of regular battalions rose from 149 in 1969, to 285 in December 1972. Some 3,000 Soviet advisors and technicians also supported the expanding PAVN along with dozens of Chinese, Cubans and other Warsaw Pact personnel.

However, for all the North Vietnamese expansion and modernization, the South had one clear superiority – its air capabilities. The Vietnamese Air Force (VNAF) had more than doubled its size under guidance from America, increasing to nine tactical wings; 42,000 personnel; and nearly 1,000 aircraft, including A-1 and A-37 ground attack aircraft; and F-5A fighters – but most at all, the South Vietnamese could still count on vital American air support from

For the first time the North Vietnamese planned a nationwide offensive by deploying a great number of armored vehicles, with more than 700 tanks and self-propelled guns engaged, most being the T-54s and Type 59s. (PAVN)

These PAVN T-34-85 tank crews take a break with the workers and families at a collective farm following a training exercise there in 1971. (PAVN)

within the country, from Thailand, or reinforced from the Pacific and the United States itself. The role played by US airpower against North Vietnam (Operation Linebacker and Linebacker II) is outside the scope of focus here, which only deals with ground operations taking place in South Vietnam. These air offensives are noted by brief summaries so the reader can gain a strategic picture of the campaign.

North Vietnam was administratively divided into four military regions, whilst South Vietnam was organized into five military regions and subsequently into Military Theaters (Fronts): the B1 Front covered the coastal zone expanding from Da Nang to Cam Ranh; the B2 Front covered the COSVN operational area; the B3 Front covered the Central Highlands area; the B4 Front covered the DMZ to the Hai Van Pass, south of Hue; and the B5 Front covered the DMZ itself and the southern part of North Vietnam. Geographically the war was mostly fought on three distinct areas: the northern part of South Vietnam, where the North Vietnamese attacked across the DMZ and from Laos; the Central Highlands; and the area north of Saigon, with strong guerrilla activity in the Mekong Delta Area. For clarity, each battle area is treated separately even if many battles are taking place simultaneously. Also, after devoting much of Volume 1 to the battles taking place in the northern part of South Vietnam in the area between Hue, Quang Tri and the DMZ, this volume focuses on the operations in the sector north of Saigon as well as in the Central Highlands.

CHAPTER 2
HANOI'S STRATEGIC SURPRISE

The North Vietnamese invasion across the DMZ caught US and Vietnamese commanders completely by surprise. They were indeed fully aware that Hanoi was planning a full-scale offensive but no-one could agree on its date nor target. The previous months had certainly seen an upsurge in North Vietnamese operations but a consensus opinion was formed amongst the intelligence communities that Hanoi would do nothing more than attack the Central Highlands On 29 April 1971 it was even hypothesized that Hanoi would wait for the US presidential election of 1972, or even until all US troops had left the country, before attempting anything. Also, the intelligence organizations consistently underestimated the new capacity of the PAVN in both motorized and armored warfare, and had therefore been unable to 'predict' North Vietnamese intentions for months. Even the commander of the MACV, General Creighton W. Abrams, shared the opinion of South Vietnam President Nguyen Van Thieu, that Hanoi would wait before attacking.

South Vietnamese intelligence was also weakened by the lack of a centralized structure even though in theory Lieutenant General Cao Van Vien was in command of the ARVN Joint General Staff (JGS). However, because military and political systems were interwoven, all power was in the hands of President Thieu – and it was the President himself who directly dealt with the four Military Regions and Corps commanders. Therefore, even if the stumbling intelligence agencies had been warned of an imminent threat, the lack of coordination and cooperation would have hindered any ARVN response. Highlighting this is the fact that, despite an intense air interdiction campaign along the Ho Chi Minh Trail, the North Vietnamese succeeded in deploying a great part of their army almost undetected. It was actually PAVN Commander-in-Chief, Senior General Vo Nguyen Giap, who decided to halt their own advance because of logistical difficulties and the threat of US airpower. With all this going unnoticed, confidence built and led to Senior General Giap's decision to send the main thrust of his campaign across the DMZ due to its location just over the North Vietnamese border. For both political and military reasons, Senior General Giap decided to open two other fronts, first to force the ARVN to disperse its limited central reserve made up by the Airborne and Marine Divisions, and second to tie down the other regular forces. Politically, he wanted to occupy as much territory as possible so North Vietnam would be in a strong position at the ongoing negotiations in Paris. Cleverly, Senior General Giap had also deduced

The North Vietnamese offensive goaded the Nixon administration to resume the air campaign, which had been suspended since November 1968. These F-4Ds from the 435th TFS of the 8th TFW head North for another mission. (USAF)

An A-7E from the VA-22 of the USS *Coral Sea* is seen being loaded with Mk-55 aerial mines following President Nixon's orders to mine the Haiphong Port, as well as the less important harbors of North Vietnam. (US Navy)

An A-7E Corsair II from the VA-195 pulls out from a bombing-run on the Hai Duong Railway Bridge on 10 May 1972. The American air attacks on the communication networks thwarted much of the North Vietnamese logistical efforts. (US Navy)

ARVN 'underestimation' of the PAVN and therefore that they would most likely expect an attack across the Central Highlands because this was the most logical attack point – being the second most important Front after the DMZ itself – so he did the exact opposite, attacking at the heart of the ARVN. To do this he heaved the PAVN directly into ARVN Military Region III, which encompassed the Saigon area, raising the stakes which he knew would catch the Americans and ARVN by surprise. He ideally wanted to seize a provincial capital close to Saigon and make it the seat of the COSVN and thus for the Viet Cong and of the Provisional Revolutionary Government (PRG) – creating a stronghold where they geographically faced, and could attack, Saigon.

The organizational drive for this campaign was massive and the reinforcement of the units within the B2 Front took top priority. The North Vietnamese requested an additional delivery of some 9,000 trucks from the Soviet Union, and 3,000 more from China to fulfil their battle needs. This effort was supervised by the Logistical Group 559 that oversaw the Ho Chi Minh Trail, which transferred enough equipment for the four main divisions at the B2 Front. From October 1971 to March 1972, some 47,500 tons of supplies were delivered, including 19,000 tons of rice. It was estimated that these deliveries would sustain troops for a three-month mechanized campaign, whilst the rice would last three months longer as they approached the gates of Saigon.

The American response

Initial US response to the offensive across the DMZ was confused and lackluster, and the Pentagon was not unduly alarmed with both the US Ambassador and General Abrams both out of the country. Also, President Nixon's first reaction to consider a three-day attack by B-52 bombers on Hanoi and Haiphong was considered too strong by his National Security Advisor, Henry Kissinger, who convinced the President to reconsider. The Americans were in somewhat of a stalemate because they did not want to jeopardize the ongoing negotiations of the Strategic Arms Limitation Treaty (SALT I) with the Soviets, whilst the need to utilize the available B-52s in coordination with the ARVN units was not always easy. However, with the increasing threat and 'squaring-up' of the North Vietnamese,

decisions had to be made and action taken – thus on 4 April President Nixon authorized the bombing of North Vietnam just above the DMZ and up to the 18th Parallel under the name 'Freedom Train'. In doing this, President Nixon knew he was taking a risk as he was due to meet Soviet Premier Leonid Brezhnev at a summit, but he weighed his options and went ahead with a very forceful air campaign – lifting most of the assault 'restrictions' associated with the Rolling Thunder Operation (1965–1968). He considered plans proposed by the Joint Chief of Staff too weak and instead ordered a massive reinforcement of air assets and pushed for the most vigorous action possible, as soon as enough combat aircraft had arrived at the given theater. He requested that the Pentagon 'get on board' and revise all plans, focusing instead on earlier studies – Pruning Knife Alpha and Duck Hook – which dated back to when he first took office in 1969. These offered far more aggressive alternatives and removed most restrictions, including the ban of attacking Hanoi and Haiphong directly, as well as the mining of North Vietnamese harbors. On the diplomatic front, the Americans suspended all ongoing negotiations in Paris as well as the secret meetings going on behind the scenes.

However, due to the continuing withdrawal of American forces, the number of combat aircraft stationed in South East Asia was less than half of its peak strength in 1968–1969, and action needed to be taken

North Vietnamese engineering units became adept at quickly repairing and building new pontoon bridges to replace those destroyed by the airstrikes. One of the techniques used was to build submerged bridges to escape air detection. This column of ZIL-130 and ZIL-157 trucks crosses over one such submerged overpass. (PAVN)

The main roads in the southern part of North Vietnam were especially targeted by American aircraft, making any trip a very dangerous undertaking. The PAVN driver of this Czech-built Praga V3S truck adjusts this ironic road sign before turning into a branch of the Ho Chi Minh Trail in Laos, for a rough and eventful journey. (PAVN)

The allied airmen faced a strong air defense system and these PAVN artillerymen make use of a 37mm anti-aircraft gun. Note the different steel helmets being used, including Chinese and Romanian variants. (PAVN)

quickly to increase this number. In fact, at the beginning of 1972, the USAF had only three squadrons of Phantoms; one A-37Bs and 76 fighter-bombers stationed in South Vietnam, whilst only another 114 fighters were located at bases in Thailand, and 83 B-52 bombers based at U Tapao, Thailand, and Andersen in Guam. Even the US Navy's Task Force 77 had only four aircraft carriers assigned to it – but usually no more than two were actually available at any one time. The USAF immediately set about changing this by sending 176 F-4D/Es and 12 F-105Gs from bases in South Korea and the United States to Thailand between 1 April and 11 May in Operation Constant Guard. Between 4 April and 23 May, during Operation Bullet Shot, the Strategic Air Command (SAC) dispatched 124 B-52s to Guam bringing the total B-52 strength to 209. The USAF continued to deploy additional units, including a wing of F-111As and one of A-7Ds throughout the summer, bringing the number of Phantoms to over 400 whilst several

squadrons of C-130 transports also arrived from the Philippines and Taiwan. The Navy also cut short recreational leave on the carriers *Kitty Hawk* and *Constellation* and ordered *Midway* and *Saratoga* to join them along with the carriers *Coral Sea*, *Hancock*, and *America*. The local 7th Fleet assets thereby increased from 84 to 138 ships, with the USMC dispatching an air wing to Nam Phong in Thailand and additional squadrons of F-4s and A-4s. In only a few months, over 1,400 American combat aircraft were available.

Now under pressure to deliver what he had promised Congress, President Nixon pushed still harder for these determined air strikes, with the first B-52 attack against North Vietnam taking place just

The North Vietnamese logistical preparations began as early as the second part of 1971 by smuggling men and equipment. These heavily camouflaged Chinese CA-10 trucks have just set off on their long and dangerous journey South. (PAVN)

One of North Vietnam's greatest achievements was the deployment of armored vehicles over great distances without being spotted. These T-54s from the 20th Tank Battalion of the 26th Armored Group are seen travelling down the Ho Chi Minh Trail heading towards their position, 80km north of Saigon. (PAVN)

The 559th Logistic Group ran the Ho Chi Minh Trail and made remarkable achievements in forwarding men and equipment to the South despite incessant air attacks. In order to protect truck drivers as much as possible, specialized equipment was issued to them. This included steel helmets like these Soviet and East German models, and Soviet 6B2 flak jackets. (PAVN)

The F-4Es of the 34th TFS from the 38th TFW operating from Korat Airbase in Thailand are being armed for another close air support sortie over South Vietnam with Mk-82 and CBU-24 bombs. (USAF)

five days after Operation Freedom Train – where in itself 12 B-52s, escorted by 53 attack aircraft, had struck petroleum storage facilities around Vinh – the most important city in the southern part of the country. On 12 April President Nixon had again reiterated his desire for more comprehensive bombings against Hanoi and Haiphong and the following day a B-52 bombed the Bai Thuong MiG base in southern North Vietnam, whilst on 16 April – in an unprecedented move – Nixon ordered a dawn B-52 attack on petroleum tank farms just outside Haiphong. This was followed by more than 100 tactical aircraft hits on targets in Haiphong and Hanoi, where subsequently four out of 17 Soviet ships docked in the North were damaged and five Soviet sailors killed. Air attacks continued to spread throughout North Vietnam – even if the B-52s were temporarily withdrawn to support the hard-pressed ARVN in the South – targeting the most strategic bridges with new laser-guided bombs. With developing ground scenarios and the need for quick targeting, President Nixon left a lot of the daily planning to local air commanders which increased efficiency. The President also seriously envisaged the bombing of the dike system that protected the Red River Delta – which could theoretically have killed over 200,000. However, apart from some accidental or isolated bombings, the dike system was never seriously damaged.

On 8 May, after much debate with senior political and military

The heavy flak encountered over South Vietnam made many VNAF O-1 and U-17 FAC aircraft very vulnerable and kept them at bay. Only the OV-10As from the 20th TASS could now operate in these zones with the 'Fast FACs'. (USAF)

Even if the North Vietnamese had installed pipelines to transfer fuel to the southern battlefields, by early 1972 they had only reached the northern part of South Vietnam. The farthest Fronts were forced to bring in fuel by trucks like this Soviet-built ZIL-157 loaded with fuel drums. (PAVN)

advisors, President Nixon ordered Operation Pocket Money, the aerial mining of the entrance to the Haiphong Harbor. In total though, 11,000 mines were laid on all North Vietnamese ports and inland waterways, effectively blocking the whole North Vietnamese coastland, but the mines were activated five days after their 'delivery' to allow enough time for foreign vessels to leave North Vietnam. However, this move caused tension with the Soviets, who mobilized their Far East Fleet to protect their eight freighters which were due in the South China Sea but, scrubbing the idea of deploying mine-hunting ships to remove the mines directly, they dispatched additional warships in the Tonkin Gulf, including an Echo I and three Echo II nuclear cruise-missiles submarines, which could threaten the American aircraft carriers directly. They were followed by the SSN-612 Guardfish that played cat and mouse during a 123 day patrol. Every available American submarine in the Pacific subsequently rushed to protect the carriers operating outside the Vietnamese waters. However, Moscow blinked first, not wanting to escalate things and jeopardise the SALT summit, pulled away and so the United States was free to act as it pleased.

With this, the number of sorties against North Vietnam rose from 400 in March to 3,485 in April, and to mark this undertaking the air campaign was duly rechristened Operation Linebacker on 9 May. The campaign now targeted enemy logistical line routes and railways; storage facilities; military installations; and the air defense system. The first objective of this renamed operation was to isolate North Vietnam from its communist allies by blocking the coasts and attacking the transhipment points at the North Vietnam–China border. Secondly, it aimed to cut off the PAVN expeditionary forces engaged in the

South. To do this, the number of sorties continued to grow and reached a record 9,344 in August with a total of 395 bridges destroyed – the mining and the air strikes combined reduced Haiphong Harbor turnover by 60 percent and over 60,000 tons of supplies were 'blocked in'. In July and August, China itself tried to orchestrate a resolution and dispatched 12 minesweepers that helped to clear a total of 46 mines in the channel leading to Haiphong. However, the obsolete Chinese Navy equipment was not up to the task and the hard-pressed North Vietnamese transportation system could only dispatch a mere 2,600 tons daily. Indeed in many areas – notably in the 'Panhandle' southern part of the country – this constant pounding of the road network reduced the delivery of supplies to a mere trickle and Hanoi's national stocks of petroleum and food had shrunk to a five-month reserve. There was an immediate impact on the battlefield as the number of North Vietnamese artillery shells dropped by half between 9 May and 11 June. However, the US intelligence community could not agree on the end-result of these shortages – some observers believed that the North Vietnamese only needed enough stockpiled supplies for a short campaign until the autumn. The North itself even acknowledged that between May and June only 30 percent of requested supplies actually reached frontline units. Indeed the North Vietnamese had always expected a renewal of the air campaign but even they were shocked by the intensity of the new operations. However, in the face of such bombardment they remained determined and pressed on with their offensive in the South anyway – with the opening of the two aforementioned Fronts under the leadership of Senior General Giap.

CHAPTER 3
THE OPENING SALVOS

Contrary to American and South Vietnamese intel, the next PAVN offensive after the assault across the DMZ did not occur in the Central Highlands but in MR III – the strategic area containing the capital of the country, Saigon – as well as several important military installations and headquarters such as the Bien Hoa and Tan Son Nhut airbases, plus the Long Binh base complex. This area encompassing seven provinces

was defended by the ARVN III Corps, comprised of three divisions as well as three Ranger Groups, and the 3rd Armored Brigade, with 120 M41 tanks and 345 M113 APCs, including the vehicles of the cavalry squadrons attached to the infantry divisions and those in reserve. The 25th Division was mainly deployed in the Tay Ninh Province which was the holy land of the influential Cao Dai sect, whilst the

5th Division's area of operations was mainly in the Phuoc Long, Binh Long and Binh Duong Provinces, with its headquarters at Lai Khe. The unit that would face the brunt of the offensive though was commanded by Brigadier General Le Van Hung, with an operation that focussed along the Saigon and Song Be River corridors, leading to the communist infiltrations. Finally, the 18th Division was headquartered at Xuan Loc and mainly operated in the provinces of Bien Hoa, Long Khanh and Binh Thuy. Commanding the ARVN strategic III Corps around Saigon was Lieutenant General Nguyen Van Minh who was a former airborne officer serving under the French. He was known for being a dynamic leader who had turned his 21st Division into one of the best. He himself had actually succeeded an infamous and well-regarded officer in Lieutenant General Do Cao Tri, who was killed in a helicopter crash in February 1971. Now, the commander of the III RAC was Major General James F. Hollingsworth, a veteran of two Vietnam tours having commanded the 1st Infantry Division, who was also a close friend of General Abrams: they had served together as tankers in the Second World War. Major General Hollingsworth's brash command style of preferring to lead men in battle and take charge himself, rather than managing a team of advisors, often grated with his ARVN counterparts. However, his deputy, Brigadier General John R. McGiffert, was the complete opposite, being a quiet and thoughtful artillery man, with a previous Vietnam tour with the 1st Infantry Division under his belt. He maintained far better relations with the South Vietnamese officers because he listened before acting.

Due to sub-standard ARVN intelligence, it was firmly believed that the North Vietnamese would limit their attacks from Cambodia against Tay Ninh City because this made the most logical sense. It was situated near a long-held enemy base at Duong Minh Chau (War Zone C) where the COSVN was suspected to operate. Indeed, even though the ARVN did toy with the suspicion that the PAVN may attack towards Saigon on Route 13, and conducted 'forward-defense' probes into Cambodia to thwart such moves: this practice was suspended. The new Corps commander suspended all deep incursions into enemy base areas, favoring a 'standoff defense' at the border, which was dictated by the need to reconstitute a Corps reserve by pulling back the Rangers and armor troops from Cambodia because of much heavier resistance since the end of 1971, particularly at the Dambe. This decision was green-lighted and enforced by General Abrams himself despite a growing fear of leaving the border unguarded. Consequently, the ARVN maintained only a string of outposts manned by the RF and Border Ranger troops to warn of any North Vietnamese incursion.

On the communist side, coordinating the whole effort in the southern part of South Vietnam, was Lieutenant General Hoang Van Thai, who was the head of the Central Office for South Vietnam (COSVN). Lieutenant General Thai had succeeded Senior General Nguyen Chi Thanh – often seen as Senior General Giap's main rival within the Central Military Commission (CMC) of the Politburo – when he died in July 1967. Under his leadership the offensive against Loc Ninh and An Loc, northeast of Saigon, was handed to Lieutenant General Tran Van Tra. Deputy Commander of the COSVN, Tra had been associated with operations in the area since 1963, and had led the Tet Offensive against Saigon four years previously. His deputy and political commissar was Major General Tran Do. Throughout these years, General Tra had always hoped for a 'decisive' offensive against Saigon and even though the planned offensive was less ambitious than this, he was thinking ahead and fine-tuning various scenarios which could be implemented on the battlefield against the South Vietnamese capital. He immediately realized that the main theater would be the northern sector of Route 13, the main commercial artery that linked Saigon to Snuol in Cambodia, in the Binh Long Province. Even though

The PAVN 33rd Independent Company of the 26th Armored Group used a variety of vehicles including tanks captured in Cambodia. This Chafee is seen during a diversionary attack against Tay Ninh in early April 1972. (PAVN)

The ARVN 25th Division reacted aggressively to the probes on the eastern perimeter of Tay Ninh but was pinned down and could not participate in the An Loc battle. The M41A3s of the 10th Cavalry Squadron, attached to the division, move out to counter-attack with the help of VNAF helicopters. (ARVN)

the province itself was small, it played an important strategic role for the South Vietnamese because if it was lost then the whole of Binh Duong Province would be threatened, sending shockwaves and panic through Saigon. A second area of operations was a portion of Route 22 northwest of Saigon, which would be used as a ruse to distract the ARVN around Tay Ninh, thus enabling the PAVN divisions to occupy their 'jumping-off' points.

Meanwhile, General Tra sent reconnaissance teams to survey the future battle area that spanned some 140km in length, from the Cambodian border at Tapang Robon, opposite Tay Ninh and the Bu Dop area, near Loc Ninh. The 276th and 739th Engineer Battalions had also now opened a new route of 140km that paralleled the Cambodian border to the main corridor of the Ho Chi Minh Trail. Perpendicular trails were also cut through the jungle and linked to this logistic artery. One of them was a 166km-length trail that ended near Route 13, whilst another of 214km extended close to Route 14. The main North Vietnamese units assigned to the new campaign were four Infantry Divisions, four independent regiments, one mixed artillery group of division size and one armored group of regimental size. The 5th, 7th

Route 13 ran north from Saigon to Loc Ninh on the Cambodian border and was of great importance to the South Vietnamese. An ARVN convoy, made up of M113s and a Toyota FQ15 light truck, returns from a logistical mission. (Nguyen Van Tran Collection)

The T-54Bs from the 20th Armored Battalion prepare to cross the Cambodian border in the vicinity of Snoul in early April 1972. Their appearance so close to Saigon would be a massive shock to the ARVN. (PAVN)

and 9th Divisions were also reorganized and trained in Cambodia, bringing them up to motorized-unit standards. Thus, each division received between 420–450 trucks, heavy 120mm mortars and quad 12.5mm, 14.5mm and twin 23mm anti-aircraft guns as well as teams of SAM-7s. The 1st Division was only partially re-equipped and was used as a reserve to be committed as required by either the MR III or MR IV. For the upcoming campaign it was also decided to equip the 75th Artillery Group up to divisional strength with the 42nd Artillery Regiment and its fifty-one 85mm guns, 105mm and 122mm howitzers; with the 28th Artillery Regiment and its two battalions of 107mm MRLs, and one battalion with 160mm mortars: and with the 71st Anti-Aircraft Artillery Regiment, with two battalions of 37mm guns, and one battalion with 57mm guns.

More importantly, it was also decided to create the 26th Armored Group, which consisted of the 20th and 21st Armored Battalions, coming from North Vietnam and the local 33rd Independent Company which was the first armored unit to be set up in Cochin China. It was initially equipped with only captured vehicles, mostly those from the Cambodian Army lost during the disastrous Operation Chenla II the previous year, and its motley collection of tanks only included six M24s, one AMX-13 tank, some M5 Half Tracks and an M113 APCs, in addition to a few PT-76s. However, at the core of this unit was much more firepower with the 38 T-54s of the 20th Armored Battalion (which traveled over 1,200km in a two-month journey without being detected). The 20th Armored Battalion had also brought with them 800kg of fuel and spare parts per vehicle, and amazingly none were lost during 30 air attacks. This battalion was followed by the 21st Armored Battalion which arrived at the end of February with 25 T-54s. However, this battalion had not been so lucky with two of its tanks destroyed by an air attack, another plunged into a ravine and another lost crossing a river in Laos. These losses were also partly due to the inexperience of the personnel of a quickly-raised unit which incorporated the lowly militiamen from the Ha Ninh Province. Finally, there were also 18 ZSU-57-2s added to the campaign which formed part of the 52nd Self-Propelled AA Company and a small number of BTR-50s.

The effort required to keep this scale of PAVN deployment secret – and so close to Saigon – was a massive undertaking, so much so that the ARVN and American top commanders ignored the incoming intelligence reports. They just didn't believe the PAVN could be so cunning. Indeed, enemy tanks had been spotted in Kratie, Dambe and Chup in Cambodia – whilst the Cambodian Army General Staff forwarded a report stating that around 30 North Vietnamese tanks were confirmed at Base Area 363, north of Tay Ninh. Thus, in direct contradiction to the ground intelligence of the South Vietnamese, by

early March 1972 most PAVN units were in place, dispersed within five depot areas and already supervised by the 340th, 500th and 700th Logistic Groups. Further still, there was now even enough supplies to sustain a three-month high intensity offensive carried out by 35,000 men, 3,200 trucks, 100 tanks, APCs, self-propelled anti-aircraft artillery armors, 100 guns and heavy mortars and 166 pieces of anti-aircraft guns. Hampering the ARVN further was North Vietnam's ploy to confuse them by moving the 24th and 271st Regiments to the northwest of Tay Ninh, at the end of March – and then by deploying two Viet Cong regiments to the southwest of Saigon. A divisional-sized force of the 33rd and 274th Regiments and the 74th Artillery Regiment cut Route 22, and by doing this the ARVN forces were diverted to Tay Ninh. In the meantime, General Tra would finalize his plans for an assault: first against Binh Long by the 5th Division, then further south along Route 13 against An Loc by the urban fighting-trained 9th Division. Also, the 7th Division would isolate An Loc City by occupying a portion of Route 13 further south in order to seal off the battlefield and to block any enemy counter-attack. Then once An Loc was taken and the ARVN 5th Division defeated, the North Vietnamese would set up a Provisional Revolutionary Government – approximately 90km from Saigon, where the 5th Division would either move south to reinforce An Loc, or move west to Tay Ninh to destroy the ARVN 25th Division. Trying to predict all battlefield eventualities, General Minh deployed Task Force (TF) 52 to Fire Support Base (FSB) at Dong Tam on Route 17 – 15km northwest of An Loc – in order to shield its western flank. Highlighting the seriousness of this campaign and the stakes laid down, this heavy TF consisted of two battalions of the 52nd Regiment of the 18th Division, with a combined 105mm and 155mm artillery battery.

The fall of Loc Ninh

The opening of the offensive was on 2 April when the PAVN 24th Regiment, with some M24s and the unique AMX-13 in support, attacked FSB Lac Long – 35km northwest of Tay Ninh on Route 22, held by the 1st Battalion and 49th Regiment of the 25th Division. The position was eventually overrun on 4 April after ARVN troops originally beat back two successive attacks thanks to VNAF support that destroyed two M24s. This loss however prompted the III Corps to evacuate all other exposed outposts located on the Cambodian border – with a column evacuating the Thieng Ngon outpost falling into an ambush and nearly all vehicles and several batteries of 105mm and 155mm howitzers destroyed. The Tay Ninh outlying defense positions were then further attacked by the 271st Regiment, which by now had fully immobilized the ARVN 25th Division. The ARVN defense of Loc Ninh included the 9th Regiment of the 5th Division and the 74th Border

A T-54B from the 20th Battalion passes a captured M41A3, probably from the ARVN TF 1-5, that had been captured north of Loc Ninh. The vehicle seems to be intact and has been hastily camouflaged. It probably entered service later with the North Vietnamese. (PAVN)

On 8 April 1972 the North Vietnamese overcame the last ARVN defenses at Loc Ninh. The T-54 tanks of the 20th Armored Battalion advance along the runway at the local airport where some South Vietnamese troops continued to resist. (PAVN)

North Vietnamese troops from the 5th Division capture this US Army Bell UH-1H inside the Loc Ninh perimeter. The helicopter was likely delivering supplies when it was damaged by ground fire and forced to land. (PAVN)

On this propaganda photo, the North Vietnamese T-54s are greeted by the citizens of Loc Ninh. Those of An Loc further south on Route 13 would offer a completely different kind of welcome though, with the local South Vietnamese Popular Forces militias staging fierce resistance. (PAVN)

Ranger Battalion under the command of Colonel Nguyen Cong Vinh. When news spread that the North Vietnamese had deployed tanks across the Cambodian border, it was decided to reinforce the town with the 1st Armored Squadron, minus one troop. After the squadron itself reached Loc Ninh, it hastily deployed under TF 1-5, 1km north of the Loc Tan intersection, approximately 10km north of the city. The TF was reinforced by an artillery platoon of two 105mm and eight ammunition trailers to establish a mobile FSB. The unit patrolled the border but saw nothing and was thus ordered on the afternoon of 4 April to pull back to the Loc Tan intersection. Furthermore, one troop received orders at the last moment to pull back towards Loc Ninh whilst, in the meantime, the PAVN 5th Division and the 3rd Regiment of the 9th Division crossed the Cambodian border in the vicinity of Snoul, and were heading south towards Loc Ninh. The 33rd Armored Company was sent to attack, followed by the rest of the 20th Armored Battalion. However, in doing this, they ran straight into Troop 3/1 and in a very one-sided fight, all the M113s were destroyed.

By morning North Vietnamese tanks had actually managed to close in on the Loc Tan intersection, where TF 1-5 tried to disengage but the South Vietnamese column was duly locked on at close range by the T-54s and ZSU-57-2s and the scene was carnage. Survivors managed to regroup on a small hill but when they tried to break away under air support, they were killed. Only two M113s managed to reach Loc Ninh whilst some 52 vehicles, including 16 M113s and 12 M41s, were either destroyed or disabled. Regrettably for the ARVN too, some of these captured tanks would later be repaired and pressed into service with the North Vietnamese. This first engagement also saw the North Vietnamese tanks prevail by knocking out an entire enemy armored squadron with minimum losses. As expected, the scale of their presence had spread panic amongst soldiers and civilians, with over 20 outposts held by the RF being abandoned just west of Loc Ninh. That night, North Vietnamese tanks were redeployed to various attack positions around the city. However, the 10th Company of the 20th Armored Battalion did arrive a little late after one of its T-54s became stuck in a bomb crater.

The pace of the offensive was unrelenting, and, at 0530 on 5 April, the North Vietnamese assault against Loc Ninh began with intense artillery shelling, including several 107mm MRLs. In fact, it only took until the end of the morning for the PAVN 5th Division to be in front of the city and simultaneously attack the 9th Regiment's defensive lines on the west, southwest and northwest sectors. The two PAVN regiments were supported by some 25 T-54s but, with well-placed air strikes of CBU cluster anti-personnel bombs and napalm, and along

The 26th Armored Group was reinforced during the An Loc battle by the ZSU-57-2s of the 52nd Self-Propelled AA Company. The vehicles were not only used in air defense roles but also as direct fire support for the infantry. (PAVN)

with 'priority' air support ordered for Loc Ninh – involving the F-5s and A-1s of the VNAF, USAF F-4s and A-37s and the aircraft from the carrier USS *Constellation* – the North Vietnamese were repulsed from the airstrip. In the meantime, General Hung also ordered TF-52s to mount an attack with one battalion to reinforce the beleaguered Loc Ninh garrison, whilst the 2nd Battalion had run into a strong enemy ambush near the road junction of Route 17 and Route 13. Despite firing 600 artillery rounds, the battalion was unable to dislodge the North Vietnamese and no more reinforcements would reach Loc Ninh.

Throughout the night, the North Vietnamese continued trying to infiltrate the South Vietnamese positions, but were held at bay by the fierce and precise firing of the AC-130s, directed by US advisors at a cost of one gunship. The next morning, another assault was hammered back due to excellent air support which included Cobra helicopters. However, the 9th Regiment Command Post was repeatedly hit by 75mm and 82mm recoilless gunfire, killing and wounding a number of personnel. The US regiment senior advisor, Lieutenant Colonel Richard S. Schott, was gravely wounded along with Captain Mark A. Smith. However, less injured and with very good Vietnamese language skills, Smith soon became instrumental in the effective coordination of US air support, and basically became the man in charge of the advisory effort during the Battle of Loc Ninh.

On 7 April, the PAVN 6th and 174th Regiments, supported by 30 tanks and captured M113s and a battery of 240mm MRLs, conquered the southern sector, followed by the northern sector that afternoon.

While the 20th Armored Battalion employed the more modern T-54B, the 21st Armored Battalion still had a great number of older T-54A variants. The unit would be held in reserve and deployed only at the last phase of the An Loc battle. (PAVN)

The last pocket of resistance was then quashed at the local airfield the following day by a company of T-54s, with some Type 63s and ZSU-57-2s spearheading the assault at a cost of a T-54 and a Type 63. The ARVN losses amounted to 600 killed and 2,400 taken prisoner. Six American advisors were also arrested by the North Vietnamese and Colonel Schott took his own life. PAVN losses were estimated to be 2,150 killed. Meanwhile, on the same day, the 7th Division had also enveloped the ARVN western flank before turning left and cutting Route 13, some 20km south of An Loc at Tau O, north of Chon Thanh. Helped by engineer units, the division had developed an extensive and sophisticated underground defensive system with a series of mutually-supportive fortified positions. Each main resistance center was occupied by a battalion armed with machine guns, mortars, recoilless guns and AT-3 anti-tank missiles, connected by several trenches and tunnels, extending 7km on both sides of Route 13. By exploiting the local topography, with its hilly, thick jungle and scattered marshes, they were very well camouflaged, and the supporting artillery was similarly hidden in the rubber tree plantations, as was the platoon of six Type 63 amphibious tanks being kept in reserve. Whilst Loc Ninh was under attack on 7 April, the TF-52s were ordered to move back towards An Loc as reinforcement, eventually to be used as a counter-attack force to relieve the pressure up north of Route 13. Whilst on the move, the unit fell into a series of ambushes set up by the 29th Regiment of the PAVN 7th Division and suffered heavy losses, including fourteen 105mm howitzers. Abandoning their vehicles, they walked back, supported by air strikes, whilst two OH-6 scout helicopters swooped down to rescue the surviving US advisors. Two

companies guarding an outpost at Can Le south of the city were then called back after blowing up the bridge there to block its use by enemy tanks. A sense of panic began to envelop the besieged city when the returning survivors told of their horrors: routed troops, civilians and tribesmen of the various ethnic minorities in the surrounding hills all converged on the provincial capital. Yet, whilst the most fortunate would escape on the last Air Vietnam DC-3 flights to leave the Quang Loi Airfield, this escape route also would soon be blocked by the North Vietnamese.

The perilous state of the city was highlighted when the 5th Division Commander, Brigadier General Le Van Hung, moved the unit's Command Post and set up defensive positions, and when senior advisor Colonel William Miller actually requested the evacuation of all his team. However, General Hung insisted that the advisors stay to coordinate logistical and air supports and, after reaching an agreement with Miller, he subsequently moved the Command Post from near the railway station to an old Japanese Second World War bunker which was resistant to air strikes. The presence of the US advisors became a real morale booster because the South Vietnamese knew they could thus depend on air support, logistical measures and the evacuation of the wounded. Often during the Easter Offensive, the advisors were the glue that held the ARVN units together in difficult situations by lending their expertise during complex combined arms operations. Being an advisor was no easy task, and depended on the characters of both the 'advisor' and the 'advised', with huge cultural and language barriers making stalemates sometimes unbridgeable. Too often, the advisor wanted things to be done the 'US way', whilst the South

Vietnamese often found the Americans arrogant and too self-assured, thus kicking the ARVN to the operational sidelines. From the start of this offensive the relationship between the advisor and his counterpart would play a key role due to the fact that the 5th Division commander was characterized as being 'anti-American' – though the ARVN held him in high regard, even if he did not always listen to advice.

The start of the Easter Offensive in Binh Long Province had been

a disaster for the South Vietnamese. In a matter of just a few days the ARVN had lost the equivalent of four maneuver battalions: one Armor, one Ranger, two infantry and more than one-third of TF-52, a sizeable number of RF soldiers, nearly two artillery battalions with 30 artillery tubes and over 100 vehicles and tanks: nothing seemed to be stemming the North Vietnamese tide.

CHAPTER 4
THE SIEGE OF AN LOC

On 6 April during a meeting with his Corps commanders, President Thieu decided top priority would be given to the defense of An Loc and in a public statement he ordered the city be defended until death. He wanted the III Corps to be reinforced by the 1st Airborne Brigade and the 21st Division, detached from the IV Corps, whilst the Paratroopers would clear Route 13 between Chon Thanh to An Loc where it would reinforce the city's defenses, with the additional division then being held in reserve to protect the northern approaches of Saigon. However, from the very the start this scheme was revised because the seriousness of the situation had not been fully appreciated. The 1st Airborne Brigade could not in fact advance northwards because it was blocked by a strong roadblock set up north of Lai Khe by the PAVN 7th Division. Instead, the Paratroopers were actually given the order to wait to be inserted inside An Loc. In their place the 21st Division from the Mekong Delta took over the task. It actually only took four days to fly the division into Bien Hoa Airbase where troops were swiftly moved to Chon Thanh, south of An Loc, to form a relief force. In the meantime, General Hung hastily reinforced the defense of the city by regrouping the dispersed units of the ARVN 5th Division and the 7th and 8th Regiments, but as the routes leading to the town had been cut, these troops were flown in despite an increasing flak threat. Within a week, the North Vietnamese themselves had positioned around the city with thirty-two 37mm, and sixteen 57mm AA guns along with dozens of 14.5mm and 23mm as well as SAM-7s, which began to inflict heavy damage on enemy aircraft. Thus the South Vietnamese, which relied on the Quang Loi Airfield 3km east of the town, were swiftly forced to use a small landing strip just to the northern exit of An Loc and to create two landing zones (LZ) and set up a helicopter landing area on a soccer pitch.

With the shelling of An Loc commencing as early as 7 April many inhabitants panicked and started digging trenches within or

besides their homes – looking for cover wherever they could. Local authorities distributed construction material, whilst some residents just fled south down Route 13, where they were easily targeted by communist artillery. With these ever-increasing stakes the first two battalions of the 8th Regiment boarded their Huey helicopters on 11 April at Dau Tieng Airfield in order to support embattled troops, but highlighting the intensity of the fighting. Whilst they flew-in they were met by a barrage of bullets and every LZ within the perimeter was shelled. The regiment commander was thus forced to set down in an open area 5km south of the city where the soldiers were ordered to take cover and find a secure place to hide and await orders. Luckily, the place was free of North Vietnamese and the troops could walk inside An Loc at a later stage. The rest of the regiment was brought in the next day and positioned to defend the northern sector whilst the western flank was defended by the 7th Regiment. The southern side was protected by 2,000 RF troops under Colonel Tran Van Nhut – a very able commander who had trained his militiamen well but who were themselves highly motivated and committed to defending their homes and families. This garrison was itself supported by the 51st Artillery Battalion on 105mm and a battery of 155mm but, apart from a platoon of V100s, they had no other armor. Hoping to even the odds though, General Hung distributed a great number of M72 LAW rocket launchers and had previously trained his troops within

The North Vietnamese soldiers of the 9th Division prepare to fire their 82mm mortar on An Loc. (PAVN)

A 122mm howitzer of the PAVN 42nd Artillery Regiment of the 75th Artillery Group is firing on the South Vietnamese positions inside An Loc. (PAVN)

Soldiers of the PAVN 9th Division attack the northern perimeter of An Loc after the preparatory artillery barrage lifted. Throughout the battle the arms coordination was very poor, revealing many weaknesses in North Vietnam's organization and training. (PAVN)

This T-54B was still smoldering after being disabled in the northern portion of An Loc City by the troops of the 3rd Ranger Group. It was part of a group of 15 tanks that were advancing down the city's main avenue without infantry support. (ARVN)

This tank-killer team from the ARVN 8th Regiment rejoice on the hull of a disabled T-54B of the 20th Armored Battalion. The smoke grenade served to mark the tank as already having been destroyed during an attack by Cobra helicopters. (ARVN)

'tank-hunting' teams. He decided to mix these teams with regular and regional troops, who knew their city well, and whilst each battalion selected its most courageous men to form these tank hunting teams, the local resistance helped with topography and setting up ambushes in the area.

Yet, following the North Vietnamese victory at Loc Ninh, they were unable to exploit their advantage and, just like taking Quang Tri in MRI, the PAVN were showing clumsiness, with division commanders unable to act quickly because they needed comprehensive action-plans. The armored battalions were thus placed directly under the command of the B2 Front which offset their advantage in terms of speed and firepower. Furthermore, they needed to forward supplies under very difficult conditions because their logistical preparations were being disrupted by intense air strikes. However, despite the air interdiction campaign the North Vietnamese stubbornly accelerated the pace of their next attack which occurred in the early hours of 13 April – despite the fact that some tanks of the 20th Armored Battalion and the 33rd Armored Company were late due to several B-52 attacks. At dawn, this major attack was initiated against the positions of the 7th Regiment on the southwestern sector whilst the main thrust came from the north, spearheaded by the 271st and 272nd Regiments of the 9th Division, supported

A T-54B of the 20th Armored Battalion approaches the ARVN forward defensive lines north of Quang Tri. However, the tanks quickly lost the accompanying infantry and found themselves venturing alone in the streets. (PAVN)

A North Vietnamese SA-7 operator in the area of An Loc. The use of the MANPADs made low flying very dangerous over the besieged city. (APVN)

A US Amy Bell AH-1G shot down in the vicinity of An Loc. Several Cobras of the F Battery of the 3rd Aviation Brigade, 1st Cavalry Division, were brought down whilst providing close air support flying low to destroy tanks. (PAVN)

A flight of VNAF F-5As from the 522nd Fighter Squadron of Bien Hoa are heading towards An Loc for a close support sortie. The aircraft are armed with a mixed load of 500lb bombs and napalm tanks. (USAF)

This T-54 was destroyed on the western perimeter of An Loc during the first North Vietnamese foiled assault. It was probably destroyed by ARVN infantry armed with M72 LAWs. (ARVN)

These T-54Bs were destroyed by the ARVN 8th Regiment on the northern sector of An Loc. The men painted their regimental number on the hulls in order to claim the kills and earn 50,000 piaster, around $50, for each tank destroyed. (US Army)

by the T-54s of the 6th Company of the 20th Armored Battalion and a platoon of Type 63s of the 33rd Company, which quickly overwhelmed the portion of the city held by the 8th Regiment and the 3rd Ranger Group. The North Vietnamese crushed the outpost positioned on Hill 128, north of the landing strip, and the defenses set up near the Province Governor's house and the adjacent high school, at a price of two T-54s and a Type 63. They then regrouped and waited for reinforcements and additional tanks before resuming the advance.

In the meantime, an overhead AC-130 had engaged the oncoming column on Route 13 and destroyed a T-54 and four trucks. The ARVN then set a barrage of mortar shells that dispersed the accompanying infantry. The tanks continued to move forwards alone and, at around 0730, a group of 15 T-54s headed into Ngo Quyen Street where a group of machine guns positioned on the roofs of buildings forced their crew to close the hatches, reducing their visibility further. Thus, when they reached Hoang Hon Avenue, a third T-54 was set alight by an anti-tank rocket. Small teams of tank-killers of the 8th Regiment crouched close to the immobilized column and destroyed three other T-54s with M72 LAWs. Seeing this, the other tank crews withdrew and rushed down adjacent streets firing on all suspect hiding-spots, which in turn forced many South Vietnamese soldiers to abandon their positions. It was actually three 16-18-year-old RF troops that brought the situation under control when they stood on the roof of a primary school and fired their M72s at it. The news quickly spread on the radio that 'youngsters' had destroyed a T-54 and a sense of morale came back to the panicked ARVN troops who began to fight back themselves and thus 'tank-hunting'. With this morale boost, two more T-54s were destroyed by the Rangers on the eastern sector near the old market, whilst the 7th Regiment claimed two more on the western area. Still focused though, the two lead tanks continued to advance,

The soldiers defending An Loc were reinforced by the 1st Airborne Brigade on 14 April 1972. The Paratroopers were landed by helicopters on two landing zones southeast of the town and had to fight their way into the besieged ruins. (ARVN)

In the meantime, the elite 81st Airborne Ranger Group landed on 45 Bell UH-1Hs on another landing zone farther south of the positions held by the Paratroopers. (Nguyen Van Tran Collection)

The mounting tank losses sustained by the 20th Armored Battalion led to the transferring of vehicles from the 21st Battalion still held in reserve in Cambodia. This T-54A was moving out towards An Loc. (PAVN)

By the end of April 1972, the ARVN 5th Division only held the southern part of An Loc. These soldiers anxiously await the next offensive from the roof of a building. (ARVN)

An ARVN soldier inspects a destroyed T-54. An internal explosion had blown away the turret. (US Army)

regularly stopping and firing on all ARVN positions encountered and one of them even reached the gate of the Command Post of the 5th Division. Such was the alarm, the division's deputy commander, Colonel Le Nguyen Vy, was forced to grab a M72 and try to 'take it out' but it was soon destroyed by a tank-killing team. The courage displayed by the division's deputy commander galvanized the ARVN and throughout the siege he repeatedly went with tank-killers to chase the tanks, personally destroying four tanks with M72 rockets. When air support finally arrived in the form of some Cobra helicopters, the pilots asked the ARVN to mark the already destroyed T-54s with smoke grenades. Three additional T-54s were subsequently destroyed by the gunships and another on the eastern sector by a Phantom.

Clearly, it appears that the PAVN assault was poorly coordinated between armor and infantry units but whilst the tank threat had been eliminated, the South Vietnamese were forced to abandon the northern quarters of An Loc. By midday the ARVN had managed to establish a new frontline along Trung Truc Street but in the southern sector the fighting continued to rage, with elements of the PAVN 95C Regiment breaching the perimeter supported by a platoon of T-54s. The RF troops counter-attacked viciously and by the evening the

fighting had subsided and each side consolidated their positions. The North Vietnamese grab on the northern sector of An Loc had been made at a heavy price, with 18 tanks destroyed, but the Americans had lost five Cobras in exchange. Despite the human casualties too, the communists pushed on the next day and rained over 7,000 artillery shells to provide suppressive fire on the enemy tank-killer teams. In doing this, the North Vietnamese managed to punch through the South's positions on the southwest sector, spearheaded by nine T-54s of the 8th Company of the 20th Armored Battalion and two ZSU-

These T-54Bs of the 20th Armored Battalion were disabled in the northern sector of An Loc by the troops of the ARVN 8th Regiment. Both of them were hit by M72 66mm HEAT rockets. (US Army)

A B-52D bomber dropped its load over South Vietnam during an Arc Light sortie in 1972. The 'around-the-clock' bombing by three bombers placed tremendous pressure on the North Vietnamese forces besieging An Loc. (USAF)

A North Vietnamese officer calls HQ after his stationed area was bombed by the B-52s. On many occasions the heavy bombers disrupted the North Vietnamese offensives, causing confusion amongst troops and tanks. (PAVN)

An ARVN soldier from the 8th Regiment looks over a destroyed T-54B at the end of April 1972. The tank was caught on the northern perimeter of An Loc. (US Army)

57-2s. One tank even came within 500 meters of the 5th Division Command Post before it was disabled by Cobra helicopters armed with the new HEAT rockets. All penetrators were pushed back thanks to an effective air support. An air strike hit the North Vietnamese forward ammunition depot some 10km northeast of An Loc and then operations were suspended when the South Vietnamese launched an airmobile assault 4km southeast of the town. After intense air strikes, the 1st Airborne Brigade was landed by helicopters on two LZs close to the Nui Gio Hill where a FSB had been established, with the CH-47As of the VNAF 237th Helicopter Squadron, that delivered eight 105mm howitzers. In the meantime, the elite 81st Airborne Ranger Group landed 45 Hueys with some 550 Commandos on another LZ farther south – all charged with fighting their way back inside An Loc.

Biting quickly though and not taking time to refit and regroup its units, the North Vietnamese launched another offensive on 15 April before these Commando reinforcements could reach An Loc. It began at 0430 with an intense artillery barrage which set a part of the city ablaze – and a two-pronged assault soon followed in the northern and western sectors by the 272nd Regiment supported by a column of 11 tanks. In the ensuing attack enemy pressure forced the 8th Regiment to pull back several streets, where it established a new defensive line after bitter hand-to-hand combat. In the confusion, the North Vietnamese tanks were again found without infantry support and several were destroyed by M72s in the Hung Vuong Street. A second attack then began at 1000 along the western perimeter where

A T-54B destroyed on the southwestern sector of An Loc by the ARVN 7th Regiment. (US Army)

An aerial view of the New Market area of An Loc where the ARVN resisted fiercely by erecting improvised barricades with civilian trucks and buses. A Type 63 of the PAVN 33rd Armored Company was destroyed by a tank-killing team when forced to stop at the placed obstacles. (US Army)

A VNAF A-1H of the 514th Fighter Squadron of Bien Hoa is taxiing out of its parking area for another close air support sortie in profit of the An Loc 'defenders'. The Skyraider was particularly regarded for its bomb-carrying capacity, here with 10 Mk-82 500lb bombs, and its precision attacks. (USAF)

A Cessna O-2A from the 20th TASS seen in flight over An Loc. The slow-flying USAF FAC aircraft paid a heavy price due to the increased enemy anti-aircraft artillery now in place over South Vietnam. Some nine O-2As and seven OV-10As were brought down between April and June 1972. (USAF)

the 9th Division threw the entire 271st Regiment into the battle with T-54 support. It breached the frontline and once again almost took the 5th Division Command Post, with one T-54 making it to within 100m of General Hung's command bunker, firing directly into it. The tank was destroyed by the Cobras that claimed four more before the end of the morning. Thanks to intense A-1 and A-37 air strikes, the ARVN counter-attacked on the afternoon and restored the frontlines, and a timely B-52 strike on the rubber plantation 4km west of the city destroyed an entire battalion that was moving to reinforce the 271st Regiment.

The next day, the 1st Airborne Brigade regrouped into two columns: the southern column reached An Loc without much difficulty but the northern column faced heavy PAVN fire. The 5th Airborne Battalion, marching at the head, was blocked by a regiment from the 5th PAVN Division supported by a platoon of T-54s. The column subsequently spent the rest of the day and night firmly held in place, constantly supported by well-aimed air strikes. On the morning of 16 April the South Vietnamese pressed on, overwhelming a North Vietnamese battalion entrenched near the railway embankment, and made the junction with the An Loc 'defenders'. The 1st Airborne Brigade was hastily placed on reserve ready to launch counter-attacks to support the most threatened sectors whilst the 81st Airborne Ranger Group was sent to the northern perimeter that they pushed back 400 meters during brutal hand-to-hand fighting with knives and grenades. With that last reinforcement, the number of ARVN troops inside An Loc amounted to approximately 7,500 men as well as over 15,000 civilians, besieged by 21,000 North Vietnamese (excluding the division engaged against the ARVN's rescuing forces moving from the south). Over the last five days the shrinking 2km ARVN enclave had been hit by 25,000 artillery rounds, and it would continue to receive between 1,200 to 2,000 enemy rockets, artillery and mortar rounds per day. The North Vietnamese had themselves been hit by over 2,000 air strikes during this opening phase of the offensive.

Realising that time was against them, the North Vietnamese quickly pressed on for another assault despite mounting losses and logistical problems. The 20th Armored Battalion which had been pulled back for rest was ordered to expedite the maintenance of its T-54s. The unit had already suffered heavy losses during five major engagements in three weeks but even the wounded, and the crews hit by malaria, were called back to duty. Tanks of the 21st Armored Battalion held in reserve were also moved forward in what would be a coordinated

A young ARVN soldier from a 'tank-killing' team poses with some M72 rocket launchers. (USAF)

It was decided to reinforce the air assets available at An Loc by deploying 32 Skyhawks of the Marine Air Group-12 to Bien Hoa Airbase by early May 1972. This A-4F from the VMA-211 is being rearmed for another sortie. (USMC)

The tense faces of these ARVN soldiers of the 5th Division reflects the weeks of incessant artillery shelling and vicious urban fighting. (ARVN)

attack by the 9th Division against the western and northern perimeters. The 95C Regiment would attack the northeastern sector, the 275th Regiment of the 5th Division, and the 141st Regiment of the 7th Division, would attack the eastern and southern sectors. However, the ARVN intelligence community had been pre-warned and troops were ready when the offensive was launched on 19 April. The offensive quickly neutralized the FSB atop of Nui Gio Hill – which was the only ARVN remaining artillery position – and the battery on the hill was quickly neutralized by the PAVN guns and heavy mortars where the 105mm were destroyed. At around 0900 the positions held by the 6th Airborne Battalion around the hill were attacked by the 1st Regiment of the 5th Division and the 142st Regiment of the 7th Division, and supported by the 10th Company of the 20th Armored Battalion. The first assault took place on the northern and northeastern perimeters where four T-54s climbed uphill alongside the infantry following a

narrow trail in thick undergrowth where, for a short time, the lead tank became stranded between two trees. The Paratroopers waited until 50m before opening fire on the assault-waves and two T-54s lay dead in the barbed-wire whilst the infantry were forced to withdraw. Another assault an hour later finally overran the position and the last two tanks were also destroyed, but three other T-54s were sent up a very steep trail whilst the remaining tanks positioned at the base of hill covered their advance. The surviving Paratroopers escaped via the steep ravines but only 106 of them would later be located and picked up by rescuing helicopters, with the others retreating into the An Loc southern perimeter.

Meanwhile, the PAVN 9th Division had launched a diversionary

The Rangers of the 3rd Ranger Group, positioned on the An Loc eastern perimeter, charge during a South Vietnamese counter-attack. (US Army)

The North Vietnamese occupied most of the northern part of An Loc which served as a springboard for most of the attacks against the South Vietnamese enclave entrenched in the southern portion of the city. (PAVN)

A North Vietnamese sniper aims with his Mosin Nagant rifle. The snipers constantly harassed the besieged South Vietnamese military and civilians inside An Loc, particularly the Drop Zone where people went to retrieve the parachuted supplies. (PAVN)

The North Vietnamese had ringed An Loc with anti-aircraft guns, making parachute drops of air support and supplies very costly. These 37mm AA guns were positioned on the hills east of the city. (PAVN)

attack on the northern sector with the last three T-54s of the 6th Company of the 20th Armored Battalion but they could not advance far when two of the tanks fell into deep bomb craters. The tanks were abandoned there when Cobra helicopters dived down to attack and once again the continuous air strikes had disrupted the PAVN timetable. It took three days to shift the effort toward the southwestern sector where the PAVN 5th Division's assault was supported by the T-54s of the 10th and 18th Companies of the 20th Armored Battalion and the Type 63s of the 33rd Armored Company. The 21st Armored Battalion was deployed on the second line, ready to exploit any breaches in the enemy's front but, right from the start, the ARVN did not give up and the RF soldiers fought particularly well under the leadership of their aggressive commander, Colonel Nhut. The stiff resistance was further bolstered by two newly deployed 5th and 8th Airborne Battalions. Another attack though developed along the southwestern perimeter where the North Vietnamese tried to infiltrate in the adjacent streets, advancing with tanks while some ZSU-57-2s positioned at a nearby rubber tree plantation, laying down covering fire from buildings. Despite that support, the PAVN infantry was pinned down by machine gun nests installed in the ruins but an isolated group of three T-54s penetrated into the 5th Airborne Battalion sector. By 23 April the second attempt to take An Loc had failed when the lead tank of a splinter tank-group was destroyed by an XM-202 and the others by the rockets of the M72s. The fighting abated until 30 April when the PAVN again attacked the northern and western sectors but with no tanks – and with massive B-52 air strikes; the ARVN prevailed again. During urgent tactical requirements the B-52 bombers were also redirected to drop their bombs within 500m of the South Vietnamese lines, and throughout April the B-52s flew 363 sorties around An Loc, dropping some 8,119 tons of bombs. Clearly both sides were exhausted but the siege nevertheless continued with the communists pounding South Vietnamese positions, whilst they themselves were under day and night air attacks.

Sustaining the siege

The battle abated somewhat with the South Vietnamese still firmly holding the southern part of An Loc whilst the North Vietnamese were in the ruined northern quarters. The opponents were now just separated by the main downtown boulevard and for three months an intense and vicious battle ensued in the devastated city with the North Vietnamese continuing to tighten their grip. Taking advantage of their gains in the northern half of the city, they installed anti-aircraft weapons on the roof of high-rise buildings to shoot incoming aircraft and,

although most of these anti-aircraft positions were quickly destroyed by American fighter-bombers, the aggressive use of anti-aircraft assets indicated that the PAVN was determined to isolate and strangle An Loc. In fact, the North Vietnamese artillery continued to maintain a high-pressure presence despite obvious American air superiority. The PAVN continually moved their guns between camouflaged positions and deployed them in depth, keeping gun tubes in reserve to replace those destroyed. The observation planes had difficulty locating the guns because they stopped firing when they were overhead and it was harder still to locate them in the open. The North Vietnamese also put to good use all their captured equipment, which included an important

A PAVN ZPU-4 14.5mm quad heavy anti-aircraft machine gun opens fire on approaching helicopters. (PAVN)

These North Vietnamese soldiers inspect the wreckage of a downed US Army OH-6 observation helicopter near An Loc. (PAVN)

The air evacuation of casualties was sporadic at An Loc due to the intensity of the anti-aircraft fire. Landing areas were quickly placed under artillery fire, causing panic and chaos among the wounded and civilians awaiting evacuation – as shown here with a VNAF Huey helicopter. (US Army)

The USAF lost five C-130Es during the parachute supply drop missions over An Loc. This Hercules was shot down on 18 April 1972 but, miraculously, the crew walked away and were picked up by rescue helicopters. (USAF)

stock of 2.75inch aerial rockets for US Army helicopters found on the Quang Loi Airfield; they were turned on their 'owners' by the use of improvised launchers. As the enemy shelling continued without rest, the conditions in An Loc deteriorated because everyone was being forced to live underground as most buildings had been destroyed and the city reduced to mounds of rubble. An Loc was strewn with trees, garbage and, worse still, the dead; and even if every effort was made to bury people in mass graves, the continuous bombing and shelling meant these corpses were being thrown back up, which meant the burial process would be re-played many times. The situation was fast becoming unbearable and dangerous, with disease now also a major problem with soldiers and residents being forced to live together in basements and bunkers. Supplies were also running very low and on 25 April the city hospital was even destroyed, meaning no medical treatment was available for over 2,000 military-wounded and countless civilians. Casualties had to be treated in the open air which itself caused more fatalities or added further injuries. The American advisors actually blamed the VNAF who were in charge of the medical evacuations for these failings – but the US Army helicopters actually fared no better themselves, only making occasional critical pickups because of the sustained flak.

By now, supplies were forced to be made by parachute at 700ft by VNAF transports despite intense anti-aircraft fire. Feeding between

23,000–27,000 people became a true challenge for the crews and it was estimated that 200 tons of daily supplies were necessary to sustain them. The American advisors estimated that the civilian population could survive with just 65 tons daily but this was about a third of what had been previously estimated. The supply situation did however improve, though those 'gathering' the supply-bundles would immediately come under sniper and shelling attack, whilst the parcels themselves would also be targeted mid-air, as the North Vietnamese did not want them to land and the South did not want the parachutes to drift towards enemy lines. However, from 13 to 16 April a total of 27 sorties dropped 135 tons of supplies into An Loc whilst only 34 tons were actually collected because the rest fell into enemy-controlled areas. However, it wasn't until two C-123Ks and one C-119G were brought down that the American C-130s were pressed into service – though initially the USAF did not fare any better, even using a new computerized dropping system known as CARP (Computerized Aerial Release Point). With this system, the pilots were instructed to follow Route 13 and as they were approaching the soccer field the computer would then take over, releasing the cargo at the prearranged point. This technique put the aircraft within range of the flak though and the precision of the cargo drops was only slightly improved. By 20 April, the USAF reverted to low-altitude drops where the C-130s would approach the city at tree-top level and at a distance of three miles from the Drop Zone (DZ) where they would climb to about 500ft and release the supplies through the rear cargo door. This tactic was relatively safe but about 70

The USAF began to drop supplies via the high altitude low opening (HALO) technique from May 1972 onwards. This saw a substantial decrease in the number of C-130Es being hit while parachuting above most of the North Vietnamese anti-aircraft gun ceilings. (USAF)

The northern, occupied part of An Loc was also fiercely bombed by American and VNAF aircraft. North Vietnamese troops were forced to live underground by digging deep shelters. (PAVN)

percent of the supplies landed outside South Vietnamese-controlled areas. After a Hercules was shot down on 26 April it was then decided to only drop supplies at night and thus accuracy remained a problem. Moreover, not many ARVN soldiers volunteered to search for errant bundles under relentless enemy artillery shelling. Some attempts were made to drop supplies with the 'high altitude low opening' (HALO) technique but with disappointing results due to the inexperience of the Vietnamese personnel packing the parachutes. After a third crash on 4 May all deliveries were suspended but the situation improved when a team of USAF specialists arrived from Okinawa and Taiwan to help pack parachutes for the HALO missions. Some 230 HALO sorties were subsequently flown, delivering a total of 2,984 tons of supplies and the garrison recovered 2,735 tons, or about 90 percent of supplies dropped, whilst the average success rate during the entire siege was only a third. The USAF 374th Tactical Airlift Wing in this same period made 57 low-level and 90 mid- or high-level drops in 305 sorties, losing five C-130s with 57 being damaged; 17 crew members were killed or missing in action; and another 10 were wounded. Despite the flak, the VNAF C-123s continued to fly 96 additional sorties and a centralized 'supplies collecting and distribution' system was introduced by the tough commander of the 1st Airborne Brigade, Colonel Le Quang Luong. The bundles were collected by hand and loaded onto all available motor transportation with food and medicines being shared among soldiers and civilians. In many cases, notably in the sectors held by the RF or the Airborne Rangers, the soldiers took great care of the local residents.

The North Vietnamese high tide

In order to break the stalemate, the B2 Front had now reorganized its forces for the third attempt to take An Loc. The more it waited, the more the aerial campaign took its toll on its depleting forces. Furthermore, even if it advanced only slowly, the ARVN relief column coming from the south along Route 13 was pressing on. The South Vietnamese even made an air assault 10km south of An Loc, near Tan Khai, and installed an FSB manned by a battalion of the ARVN 9th Division, and whilst this base was soon to be encircled, it resisted stubbornly and provided much needed artillery support. This spurred General Tra to resume the offensive, but the badly shaken 9th Division reverted to a more supportive role by continuing to hold the northern part of An Loc, yet still being forced to endure a horrendous pounding by the allied aircraft. The main attack would now be handed over to the 5th Division – with its 6th, 174th and 27th Regiments concentrated against the southwest sector – and one regiment of the 7th Division left at the Tau O Creek to 'watch' the ARVN relief column, and the 165th and 141st Regiments were positioned on the southeast sector. The inexperienced 21st Armored Battalion that had just completed its training in Cambodia would finally enter the fray in support of the badly depleted 20th Armored Battalion, whilst some 16 additional Type 63s that arrived from the Ho Chi Minh Trail were given to the 21st Armored Battalion, bringing its strength to 36 tanks, and the 33rd Independent Armored Company saw its ranks bolstered by a platoon of BTR-60s and was redirected towards An Loc. It left only some captured M24s and M41s to support the operations along Route 13, whilst the tanks were now placed directly under the control of the B2 Front, rather than being placed with the involved divisions, in order to improve combined-arms tactics.

The 21st Armor Battalion, which had been held in reserve in Cambodia, is now redirected towards An Loc to take part in the last attempt to take the city in May 1972. (PAVN)

As a last effort, the North Vietnamese launched a third attempt to conquer An Loc on 11 May 1972. They committed all their remaining tanks, including 16 additional Type 63s just arriving from North Vietnam. (PAVN)

This Type 63 was destroyed during an attack on the An Loc western sector. It was hit by an M72 LAW rocket in the Phu Lo Quarter. (US Army)

It was at this point that the ARVN and Americans started to doubt themselves because even though this impending attack was known of in advance – by SIGINT collections, ARVN patrols and prisoner interrogations – they had little confidence in withstanding a third push. Allied commanders even knew the exact timing and the targeted areas but still action needed to be taken. It was then that General Abrams made the massive decision to cancel all scheduled B-52 strikes and exclusively hone them in on An Loc. The bombers would thus only attack tactical targets on the frontlines and not the enemy's logistical organization, as was the case previously. This would translate to a B-52 strike every 55 minutes over a 24-hour period. Expecting criticism he ordered the same bombing-procedures the next day for MR II then MR I.

Inside An Loc the 5,700 South Vietnamese troops were becoming even wearier and their morale was shattered after weeks of fighting without rest under incessant shelling. Some attempts were made to reinforce the garrison by VNAF helicopters but were soon suspended due to the heavy flak that brought down a CH-47. The mental stress was taking its toll on the Americans too, and on the eve of the new offensive an exhausted Colonel Miller was replaced by Colonel Walter Ulmer in a daring helicopter pick-up operation. It was also becoming glaringly obvious that the relationship between General Hung and Colonel Miller had reached a low tide that would impact unfavourably on command decisions. Then just two days after switch in personnel, the North Vietnamese finally unleashed their offensive on 11 May. It took place amongst a fury of B-52 and fighter-bomber attacks whilst working side by side with his counterpart, General Lam – the Senior III Corps advisor – and General Hollingsworth, coordinated the air strikes. Often flying over the battle scene and speaking directly to the American advisors and the ARVN commanders inside the city,

During the last phase of the An Loc battle, the North Vietnamese even sent in their ZSU-57-2 anti-aircraft tanks as direct fire support. This vehicle was destroyed on the eastern perimeter. (USAF)

The main attack axis during the last North Vietnamese offensive against An Loc was aimed at the southern sector of the city. A Type 63 from the 21st Tank Battalion that was supporting the PAVN 271st Regiment of the 9th Division was destroyed in that sector. (ARVN)

the generals readjusted the 18 Arc Light 'boxes' (the name given to the areas targeted by three B-52s, each covering roughly a length of 3km and a width of 1km), around An Loc and added seven more. Numerous Forward Air Controller (FAC) planes orbited the area, directing the waves of fighter-bombers and helicopters, often stacked at various altitudes by waiting their turn to attack. The F-4 Phantoms operating from Thailand adopted a new operational procedure which meant they released their bombs before landing at Bien Hoa for rearming. After this they would then fly two more attack sorties from Bien Hoa before completing one last sortie and returning to Thailand, thus fully exploiting their time over the operational zone rather than losing it by long transit flights.

However, the North Vietnamese themselves kept pushing on with coordinated tank-infantry assaults where they fired over 17,500 artillery rounds within 12 hours. They also moved in additional 23mm and 37mm anti-aircraft guns to provide cover from air attack but also to give direct support-fire. All the sectors of the South Vietnamese enclave were then attacked simultaneously as the PAVN was determined to push towards the center of the city where they could link up and split ARVN forces into smaller pockets, to be destroyed one by one. Yet having seemingly not learnt from previous attacks, the 40 tanks assembled for that assault were again dispersed amongst the five regiments involved, and not concentrated along a single main axis of attack in order to exploit their 'shock and awe' prowess. The main attacks focussed on the western and north-eastern sectors where the perimeter was breached and the ARVN initially faced the 272nd Regiment of the 9th Division supported by three T-54s, two Type 63s and the 6th Regiment of the 5th Division who were themselves accompanied by three T-54s and one Type 63. The small tank groups were sent first to probe the enemy defenses and to determine which streets could be taken by the other tanks which waited concealed in the rubber tree plantations. On the western side, two T-54s rolled over an improvised mine – made of two 155mm artillery shells tied together with a detonator – and were blown up. The third T-54 that tried to bypass the burning hulls fell into a bomb crater and was immobilized. Only the two Type 63s reached the Phu Lo Quarter but were immediately destroyed by ARVN tank-killing teams armed with M72s. The communist thrust along that sector was finally contained when their promised armored company was not on schedule due to its parking area having been devastated by a B-52 strike. On the northern perimeter the 274th Regiment attacked the positions held by the 81st Airborne Ranger Group and soon benefited from the support of a

second group of tanks sent in reconnaissance, but all the three tanks were finally destroyed at close range by the M72s near the Chinese High School.

Another platoon of T-54s now took over and carefully drove south through the maze of destroyed buildings and burned out vehicles. The advance continued when 10 additional T-54s punched through the lines held by the ARVN 8th Regiment. They advanced methodically, covering one-another supported by several ZSU-57-2s that rained down a barrage of 57mm shells on each crossroad. The ARVN was forced to fall back until Nguyen Trung Truc Street where tank-killing teams were positioned on rooftops and quickly destroyed four T-54s. Two others were then attacked from the rear by South Vietnamese soldiers who had rushed through specially made creep-holes in the walls of the destroyed buildings. However, a communist battalion succeeded to entrench itself near the new market between the 8th Regiment and the 81st Rangers – and a group of T-54s soon rolled up in support, inflicting severe damage and killing many South Vietnamese counter-attackers. The seriousness of the situation was so, that within less than 20 minutes a flight of B-52s was diverted from its intended target outside the city and directed over the zone. The bombs fell less than 600m from the ARVN positions in an incredible display of American firepower; the situation on the north-eastern sector was then stabilized and a battalion of Paratroopers counter-attacked.

Yet, the main North Vietnamese effort was taking place in the southern sector where they engaged the 271st Regiment of the 9th Division – and in the second phase – the 275th Regiment of the 5th Division. They were supported by a company of 12 T-54s preceded by a platoon of Type 63s sent first to scout, but the leading tank was, however, destroyed by the RF troops. The others pushed on and reached the Xa Cam Quarter which was being weakly defended by the survivors of the TF-52. The tanks were then ordered to attack the ARVN 5th Division Command Post which was coordinated with the 272nd Regiment and attacked from the western sector, and at around 1000 the South Vietnamese began to cede, with the 3rd Battalion of the 7th Regiment forced to pull back. But at that moment the communist troops made a grave mistake: constantly attacked by the Skyraiders and the Cobras and caught in vicious street fights, many platoons sent in to reconnoitre the way leading to the objective became disoriented and lost, thus incorrectly attacking the Provincial Public Work Building 300m away from the enemy Command Post. When a few scouts realized their mistake, they honed in on their 'real' target but the situation appeared desperate until the 5th Division commander

This T-54B was found abandoned near a bomb crater in the southern sector of An Loc. The constant pounding by attack aircraft and B-52 bombers had turned the surroundings into a chaotic landscape that made tank deployment difficult. (Nguyen Van Toan Collection)

A column of T-54Bs destroyed in the sector held by the ARVN 8th Regiment at the end of May 1972. (ARVN)

North Vietnamese drag their anti-aircraft guns to the front in order to provide fire coverage for their assaulting troops. This 37mm gun was captured by the ARVN Rangers. (ARVN)

promptly reacted. He sent the 5th Airborne Battalion from the south of the city to the endangered areas, with General Hung even announcing that he would rather commit suicide than be taken prisoner. As the situation became perilous though, it was becoming clear to the ARVN that the North Vietnamese planned to cut An Loc in half with a pincer movement of two main attacks in the north-eastern and western sectors. The Paratroopers thus moved in and saved the situation by stopping the enemy advance. Furthermore, the 1st Airborne Brigade ordered the 8th Airborne Battalion to counter-attack to recapture the Xa Cam Gate area in the south in order to seal off the arrival of further PAVN reinforcements. The attached American advisors superbly guided a series of air strikes carried out by the VNAF A-1s and USAF A-37s, dropping 250lb bombs and, despite the introduction of the new SAM-7s over the battlefield, the Cobra pilots courageously dived in to attack the tanks. By noon, the assault was broken, with five T-54s and one BTR-50 destroyed but at the cost of four airplanes and two AH-1G helicopters. Continuing in the same vein throughout the day, the North Vietnamese were constantly pounded by aircraft that flew a record 297 tactical sorties in addition to 30 B-52 strikes. The effect was immediate and the communists were unable to make further progress, and over these two days the ARVN counted an additional 23 tanks destroyed inside their perimeter.

Over the next four days some 260 sorties were flown each day while the AC-130 gunships orbited to provide precise cover-fire for ARVN troops – but despite all this the North Vietnamese renewed their attack on 12 May. In the western sector, combat turned to hand-warfare when the North Vietnamese infantry of the 272nd Regiment surged forwards after the lifting of the artillery barrage. The 81st Airborne Ranger Group then saw a group of six T-54s moving towards them along a plantation road, Route 303, and they quickly

devised a bold scheme to halt their progress by 'knocking out' the lead tank on the bridge and thereby creating an impassable obstacle. The Rangers fulfilled their mission by sneaking to within 30m of the bridge and waited on both sides of the road with their M72s ready. Then, as the lead tank reached the middle of the bridge, six M72s hit it. The vehicle was destroyed in precisely the right spot, blocking the rest of the T-54s. In the meantime, the 174th Regiment attacked the north-eastern sector whilst supported by six T54s – but four of them were destroyed by air strikes before reaching the town's outskirts. New attacks were then quickly launched during the afternoon when North Vietnamese columns were shelled by the ARVN mortars, but the infantry dismounted from the tanks to crouch in shell holes and the PAVN then reorganized its units for a new attack. During the night, the North Vietnamese again tried to take An Loc in another desperate attempt covered by very bad weather that grounded most of the aircraft. Two attacks developed from the north and east, with Type 63 tanks in support, and with infantry only from the west and the south. However, six B-52 formations were redirected against the PAVN and caused heavy casualties. Two AC-130s took over when the weather improved and helped to break this new offensive.

Following a quieter period on 13 May, the early hours of the 14th saw increased activity when PAVN tanks attacked once again from west and southwest. The most significant activity was at 0145 when the ARVN had to deal with probes on the west and southwest – and at the same time tank fire was received. This attack was, however, broken by B-52 strikes with an entire company of tanks caught in a pre-planned B-52 target-box and completely wiped out. Taking advantage of the weakened PAVN posture, the South Vietnamese counter-attacked over the following days and, on 15 May, the 8th Regiment pushed on but encountered fierce resistance. However, two T-54s were destroyed at point-blank range by an ARVN sergeant armed with M72s. The exhausted North Vietnamese now began to loosen their grip around the city while the ARVN gradually regained most of its territory lost over the previous days, but they were still under heavy daily shelling with an average of over 2,000 rounds.

With this change in fortune, the North Vietnamese redeployed their forces south of An Loc in order reinforce their defense against the relief column that was now expected to break through after all. On the night of 19 May the North Vietnamese attacked the positions held by the 1st Airborne Brigade south of the city, but the South Vietnamese had been warned in advance and the 8th Airborne Battalion ambushed

Another T-54B belonging to the 20th Tank Battalion destroyed on the outskirts of An Loc. It was hit by an anti-tank rocket that ignited its internal ammunitions. (US Army)

the enemy tanks in the rubber plantation adjacent to their defensive positions. During the violent fighting, Paratroopers closed in and engaged the tanks with their M72s with some even jumping on the vehicles and throwing grenades through the hatches. Eight more T-54s and Type 63s were destroyed as well as some M113s captured. Various PAVN assaults were foiled but on 23 May the communists launched a last desperate effort against the southern perimeter in order to seal off any attacks by the garrison. A column of eight T-54s approached without infantry support and were immediately engaged by F-4s with 500lb bombs that destroyed or immobilized several of them, with the rest destroyed by ARVN tank-killing teams. At this point the battle may not have been won, but it was becoming obvious that the North Vietnamese no longer had the capacity to capture An Loc: the city was still under siege but firmly in ARVN hands. The North Vietnamese losses at this last stage amounted to over 5,000 casualties and some 40 tanks, whilst nearly all the committed armored force during the last offensive had been destroyed. Inside An Loc itself, the 5th Division had expanded its perimeter from 8 to 12 June and the constant air attacks had now silenced most of the anti-aircraft defense positions. The first helicopters landed on 9 June and the following day a link-up was made with the relief column coming south from Route 13; Twenty-three Hueys arrived and collected several dozen wounded

soldiers. On 13 June an additional regiment from the 18th Division was flown into the town by helicopters, with the rest of the division promptly arriving to take over from the exhausted 5th Division. The helicopter pilots of the 229th Aviation Brigade were shocked at what awaited them in the city, with many casualties too exhausted to move and cry out for help. The next day, the siege was officially declared over, even if operations continued against the blocking positions left elsewhere by the PAVN; and on 7 July President Thieu visited An Loc, awarding General Le Van Hung the National Order 3rd Class. Two days later, the deputy advisor to the ARVN III Corps, Brigadier General Richard Tallman, was killed by a North Vietnamese artillery attack on his visit to the city. He was, at that point, the highest ranking US Army officer to be killed in Vietnam.

However, even if most of the PAVN forces had been pushed back north of An Loc toward the Cambodian border, they still held Loc Ninh, and Route 13 was also still interdicted at Tau O Creek. This situation was not resolved until 20 July when the 25th Division – which had relieved the weary 21st Division – finally overwhelmed the last resistance. This firmly proved once again how resilient and determined the North Vietnamese were and how much they were willing to risk and lose for their cause.

CHAPTER 5
ORDEAL ON ROUTE 13

Whilst the North Vietnamese had tried to conquer An Loc, they were forced to divert one of their three divisions further south on Route 13 in order to seal off the battlefield and to hold back the South

Vietnamese trying to break into the offensive circle. The PAVN 7th Division may have lacked the strength to overcome the tenacious ARVN counter-attacks but their role in disrupting the South's relief efforts over four months was a remarkable defensive operation. The division had actually been specially trained in this kind of operation and had prepared well, studying the terrain and creating a network of deep horseshoe underground supporting shelters. The North Vietnamese quickly perfected this blocking tactic into what they called Chot and Kieng. A Chot usually consisted of an A-shaped 6m-deep trench, reinforced overhead, constructed on terrain that allowed for effective enfilade fire on likely avenues of approach. The Chot was categorized into 'A' (squad size), 'B' (platoon size) and 'C' (company size). The Kieng in Vietnamese means chain, or shackle, which in its military designation indicated a system of inter-connected Chots which provided mutual support. With this system of Chot and Kieng, the PAVN was able to use a relatively small force to effectively block a much larger one for a long period of time. In fact, the cut of Route 13 took place just north of Chon Thanh, the main ARVN outpost, with Lai Khe just south of An Loc at 30km away. This road also cut through the towns of Tau O, Tan Khai, Xa Cat, Xa Trach and Xa Cam. The defensive system set up south of An Loc was established along the railway running parallel to Route 13 and was hidden behind the deep marshes in the Tao O area which constituted a formidable natural barrier against attacking units moving from the south. However, the slightly elevated railway running a few hundred meters east of Route 13 provided good protection for enemy ambushing forces and the whole fortified system was linked to the rubber plantations west of Route 13 by an elaborate network of trenches that allowed supply and medical evacuation.

The first ARVN attempt to clear Route 13 took place as early as April when the 43rd Regiment of the 18th Division was ordered to secure the route north of Lai Khe; it was subjected to artillery fire but met only light resistance in comparison to other battlefields in Vietnam. Therefore, it actually arrived at Chon Thanh without much difficulty on 7 April but its attack further north the next day was stopped short despite powerful artillery and tactical air support. Indeed, the 43rd Regiment suffered a 30 percent rate of casualties and was forced to withdraw. The JGS then decided to commit the 1st Airborne Brigade in place of the regiment, but their first attack on 11 April was also a failure and they were unable to destroy the enemy blocking positions. They also suffered heavy casualties along with the attached 5th Armored Squadron which lost its commander, Colonel Truong Huu Duc.

This opening stage set the theme as their mission soon degenerated into bloody fighting, with the North Vietnamese determined to inflict as much pain and losses as possible. The ARVN III Corps for its part put top priority on freeing An Loc and containing any advance by the North towards Saigon. The battles in MR I with the fall of Dong Ha, then Quang Tri south of the DMZ (see *Volume 1*) made the South Vietnamese situation perilous and it was fast becoming merely about holding defensive lines and stemming the onslaught. The next phase of the North Vietnamese drive was becoming obvious and would take place on a national level on the different fronts. In early May, General Abrams. along with Ambassador Ellsworth Bunker, met President Thieu to discuss the ineffectiveness of ARVN field commanders, and in an unprecedented move he decided to discharge those leaders identified as being most incompetent. The Americans hoped that, by doing this, morale amongst troops would increase with the new commanders ordered to block the communist advance at all costs, particularly at Hue, Kontum and An Loc. It was well understood that if the latter city fell, the road would be wide open for a direct offensive against Saigon itself. Of the three MR-Corps commanders directly threatened by Hanoi, two were then demoted: Lieutenant General Ngo Dzu in II Corps was replaced by Major General Nguyen Van

The PAVN 7th Division's role for over four months was to block ARVN relief efforts on Route 13, which was a remarkable operation. It was supported by armor detachments of the 33rd Armored Company – mostly equipped with captured vehicles like this M41A3. (PAVN)

Toan; and Lieutenant General Hoang Xuan Lam of the I Corps was replaced by one of the best South Vietnamese commanders, General Ngo Quang Troung – currently at the head of the IV Corps in the Mekong Delta Area. Several division commanders were also removed for failing on the battlefields, or to ease the always-complicated ARVN command relationship; only Lieutenant General Nguyen Van Minh of the III Corps was saved as he had managed to stabilize the situation at An Loc after the disaster and the quick collapse of Loc Ninh. He had confronted the PAVN head on and thus as he pleaded his case with the JGS and President Thieu, he subsequently succeeded in getting the 21st Division – a unit which had previously belonged to the IV Corps in the Mekong Delta Area.

This was a remarkable departure from the static mentality that prevailed within ARVN before 1972 where tactical movement was slow and military divisions jealously guarded. The 21st Division subsequently withdrew from the mangroves of the Ca Mau area where it was conducting operations, and by 10 April its 32nd Regiment had been airlifted into Lai Khe, whilst the rest of the division, including its artillery, was moved to the Lai Khe and Chon Thanh area two days later. A great part of the 31st and 33rd Regiments had been displaced by an air bridge set up by the VNAF C-47s, C-119s and C-123s which took them to the Bien Hoa Airbase, and then trucked to the frontline. The 21st Division was also reinforced by the 9th Armored Cavalry Squadron with a troop of M41 tanks, and from 12–23 April the division consolidated its operational base in Lai Khe and organized its logistical system in preparation for its relief mission. Its troops also needed to adapt to the new battlefield of jungles and small hills as they were used to operating in the flooded rice fields, swamps, and canals of the Mekong Delta against lightly armed Viet Cong guerrillas,

The task of reopening Route 13 in order to relieve the besieged garrison of An Loc fell to the ARVN 21st Division. It was reinforced by the tanks of the 5th Armored Cavalry Squadron with these M113s which are heading north to support the drive. (US Army)

The North Vietnamese built a series of fortified interconnected blocking positions along Route 13 that proved remarkably resistant to air and artillery bombardment. Any penetration into the system led to determined counter-attacks. (PAVN)

An ARVN M113 drives at full speed to pass a dangerous stretch of Route 13 north of Lai Khe. (US Army)

but were now expected to face well-armed North Vietnamese regular divisions supported by artillery and tanks. With this deployment the division had taken over the role of clearing Route 13 from elements of the 18th Division and thus freed the 1st Airborne Brigade to be drafted into An Loc. The 21st Division made its first attack on 23 April by launching a pincer movement with the 32nd and 33rd Regiments, from Chon Thanh and Lai Khe respectively, in an effort to destroy the North Vietnamese 101st Regiment and elements of a sapper battalion that had infiltrated that section of Route 13. After five days of tough fighting the 21st Division secured the area and counted more than 600 dead North Vietnamese, whilst the ARVN in turn had lost 300 troops over a 4km stretch of railway running parallel to the route.

In the meantime, the III Corps had also been reinforced by the 3rd Airborne Brigade in order to defend the northern approaches of Saigon, and on 24 April, Chon Thanh – the Light Headquarters of the Airborne Division – was 'flown in' and placed under the command of Colonel Ho Trung Hau, so he could coordinate operations of the 1st Airborne Brigade (who were already in An Loc) and the 3rd Airborne Brigade. Colonel Hau met the 21st Division commander, Major General Nguyen Vinh Nghi, to discuss the now combined effort to clear out Route 13 and it was decided that the 3rd Airborne Brigade would clear the section of Route 13 from Tau O Creek to Xa Cam, just south of An Loc whilst the 21st Division would be responsible for the territory south of Tau O, and would provide assistance to any attacked area within its zone of responsibility. With this move it is

clear to see that the JGS feared the North Vietnamese could bypass Lao Khai by combining several independent regiments with local Viet Cong battalions and thus cut South Vietnam's logistical lines.

Indeed, it only took a day before the 3rd Airborne Brigade swung into action on 25 April as the 2nd Airborne Battalion attacked the area northeast of Tau O and another area about 1km east of Tan Khai. The battalion soon established FSB Anh Dung with a 105mm battery brought in by VNAF Chinooks which could now provide fire support for the Route 13 clearing operations and also for An Loc. However, the FSB quickly came under PAVN artillery fire and by the next day a group of North Vietnamese soldiers had broken through its fences and opened fire against the howitzers with 75mm recoilless guns. The same day, the 1st Airborne Battalion made a helicopter assault into the Duc Vinh area – about 4km north of Tan Khai – but still relying on its 'leapfrog' advance-tactic air assaults, Colonel Hau also inserted the 3rd Airborne Battalion on 2 May into an area east of Route 13 between Tan Khai and Tau O. Their mission was to widen the ARVN's control area westward and to link up with the other airborne battalions to the north. From 5–7 May they engaged in heavy combat with the North Vietnamese and both sides suffered heavy losses. It was now apparent that the North Vietnamese had developed new tactics to avoid direct Paratrooper engagement, thus minimizing their casualties; they would shadow their targets stealthily and close in to open fire. With these new techniques the 3rd Airborne Battalion quickly became 'locked down' and suffered heavy losses between 12–14 May. They were also ambushed a mere 500m of Tau O, which had a domino effect on the 1st Battalion operating in the Duc Vinh area because without their link-support they were unable to secure their own objective north of Tau O.

Similarly, on 1 May, when the 31st Regiment attacked an area 7km north of Chon Thanh, they were immediately pinned down by the PAVN 165th Regiment and elements of the 209th Regiment. The 21st Division thus hastily ordered two battalions of the 32nd Regiment to conduct an envelopment east of the enemy on 8 May but, despite massive firepower consisting of eight B-52 strikes, 142 tactical air sorties and some 20,000 rounds of artillery, the 31st Regiment was unable to remove the enemy blocking positions south of Tau O. Both

The M41A3s from the III Armored Brigade support a new attack by the ARVN 21st Division to clear out a new North Vietnamese stronghold along Route 13, just south of the Tau O Creek. (Albert Grandolini Collection)

The ARVN 21st Division's advance encountered particularly stiff resistance because each enemy blocking position – as with this one near the Phu Hoa on Route 13 – had to be taken out one by one in costly infantry assaults. (ARVN)

ARVN regiments suffered heavy losses, with over 400 casualties which included the two battalion commanders, whilst Colonel Nguyen Huu Kiem – commander of the 31st Regiment – was seriously wounded. With the deteriorating battle scene the JGS decided to remove the 3rd and 2nd Airborne Brigades from the Route 13 offensive and reinforce the ARVN's last defensive line north of Hue. The 3rd Airborne Brigade was replaced by the 15th Regiment, commanded by Lieutenant Colonel Ho Ngoc Can of the 9th Division, which was operating in the Mekong Delta. As already indicated, President Thieu had decided to change the ARVN command structure and thus Lieutenant General Ngo Quang Truong, IV Corps Commander, was appointed as the new I Corps Commander – placed in charge of the counter-attack to recapture Quang Tri (see *Volume 1*). With these changes, the President therefore directly impacted the command structure on Route 13 with the 21st Division Commander, Major General Nguyen Vinh Ngi, replacing General Truong. Colonel Ho Trung Hau – who had been in charge of the Airborne Division Light Headquarters at Lai Khe – was promoted to Brigadier General and took over the command of the 21st Division but this decision was very knee-jerk and even though he knew the battlegrounds well, his arrogance and rudeness would soon antagonise officers within the 21st Division. His American senior advisor, Colonel Franklin, would also confront him over his lack of tactical initiatives which caused unnecessary losses.

However, amid this change of command the orders given to the 21st Division did not alter and they were again soon attempting to clear out the blocking positions on Route 13 – but this time with the North Vietnamese now focusing on An Loc, they did actually make a little progress in their northward advance. Their new attack took the form of a direct assault against the entrenched enemy's defensive system by the 32nd Regiment, supported by the 6th, 73rd and 84th Ranger Battalions; and the M113s and M41s of the 5th Armored Squadron. The assault though faced massive opposition from the PAVN 209th Regiment that was deployed over a 3km front in the middle of hilly terrain and it took three days of extremely heavy fighting to defeat the PAVN blocking units which lay about 8km north of Chon Than. Finally on 13 May, the PAVN 165th Regiment was forced to pull back to new defensive positions south of Tau O Creek – but there they settled into a very deep entrenchment system, supported by the 209th Regiment – and therefore the exhausted ARVN attacking column was again forced to stop a mere 5km north at the Tau O area. It was here that the hardest and longest battle was fought, with the PAVN 209th Regiment resisting for 38 consecutive days, despite incessant B-52 strikes. With this, from 11 May–21 June General Hau chose to throw the whole of the 21st Division at the problem, who themselves were being heavily shelled by long-range artillery, and the battle soon

The North Vietnamese troops from the 7th Division take some rest and a well-deserved meal just outside their bunker. It was part of an intricate fortification system that blocked the ARVN relief column along Route 13. (PAVN)

turned into a positional trench fight and artillery duel with the ARVN counting 503 North Vietnamese killed, whilst 99 of their own troops died too – including a battalion commander. The North Vietnamese troops suffered most though, under constant pounding by air strikes at the height of summer, with little rice or water and surviving by merely 'digging in' to their trenches and rotating the watches.

On 11 May as the 21st Division was launching a new offensive north of Chon Than, the 15th Regiment of the 9th Division – reinforced with the 9th Armored Squadron – arrived in the town. In light of this, three days later the 15th Regiment became TF-15, consisting of 1/18, 2/15 and 3/15 Battalions; the 15th Reconnaissance Company, 9th Armored Squadron, one 105mm battery and one 155mm platoon. This newly constituted unit was then immediately ordered to launch an eastern envelopment by seizing Ngoc Lau, east of Route 13, which was quickly reached on 15 May. The following day 2/15 Battalion assaulted by air into Bau Nat Village, 1,500m east of Tan Khai, and linked up with the 1/5 Battalion at the above location. Afterwards, Tan Khai was turned into FSB Long Phi with one combined 105mm and 155mm battery, whilst on 17 May, the 15th Reconnaissance Company and the 3/15 Battalion air-assaulted an area northwest and west of Tan Khai respectively. The 2/15 Battalion was then ordered to link up with the 3/15 Battalion while its place at the FSB Long Phi was taken over by the 33rd Regiment. However, when the regiment moved out through the forested area it was repeatedly engaged by enemy forces and sustained heavy casualties. Within 15 days 50 were killed and 300 wounded. The ARVN efforts to push through the roadblock on Route 13 gave no tangible results and the South Vietnamese faced one of the best interlocking and echeloned fortifications of the entire campaign – set up in the deep swamps of Tau O area.

The next day despite these losses, the 9th Armored Squadron on the west, and the 33rd Regiment on the east – using Tan Khai as the line of departure – began to move northwards in an effort to bypass the Tau O area completely and to finally link up with An Loc. The PAVN 7th Division reacted by attacking the advancing TF-15 at Duc Vinh II Hamlet and by encircling and increasing the pounding of FSB Long Phi. Faced with this new threat to its rear, Lieutenant Colonel Hau Ngoc Can – TF-15 Commander – dispatched the 1/15 Battalion to reinforce the defense of the FSB which served as the logistical and medical evacuation center; there would be strong clashes for 13 consecutive days. In the meantime, its leading elements were also being heavily engaged whilst crossing the Xa Cat Creek, so Lieutenant Colonel Can ordered the units to progress in echelons so that TF-15 could secure a bridgehead over the Xa Cat Creek, but due to strong anti-aircraft fire, it had to be supplied by parachute drops. On 22 May, TF-15 finally reached an area close to Thanh Binh Hamlet where it was ferociously counter-attacked. The next day, the North Vietnamese mounted another attack supported by the Type 63s of the 3rd Company of the 21st Armored Battalion but the lead Type 63 that had broken through the ARVN lines at 0600 was destroyed by 106mm recoilless guns mounted on M113s, but the others continued. ARVN troops held their positions and soon destroyed another tank, with the North Vietnamese finally forced to withdraw when their supporting elements in Than Binh Hamlet were bombed by the B-52s. The North Vietnamese troops however closed in to less than 100m from the ARVN perimeter in order to offset the air attacks, and again the TF-15 advance was stalled.

On 24 May when the APCs of the 9th Armored Squadron were mobilized to ferry supplies, they were ambushed by the PAVN 141st

This M41A3 from 1/9th ACS, attached to the 21st ARVN Division, has just been hit by an RPG (B-40) rocket. The tank crew has just enough time to evacuate the smoking vehicle that soon burns out completely. (Albert Grandolini Collection)

An ARVN 105mm howitzer blasts away to cut down North Vietnamese infantry counter-attacking south of the Tau O Creek in May 1972. TF-15 suffered heavy casualties in the last drive towards An Loc. (ARVN)

Regiment from well-prepared positions that housed Type 63 tanks and tank-killing teams with RPGs and AT-3 missiles. An entire troop of the 9th Armored Squadron was wiped out, with 22 M113s also put out of action, but despite this TF-15 pressed on northwards the next day against fierce resistance anchored in well-camouflaged bunkers. In the meantime, the 33rd Regiment moving from Dong Phat Hamlet towards An Loc was also stopped by the PAVN 165th Regiment which occupied a well-prepared defensive sector at the Xa Cam rubber plantation 4km south of An Loc. The ARVN III Corps requested B-52 strikes against this new formidable defense structure but US advisors would not 'waste' ammunition. The request though was forwarded to the VNAF that proposed to attack it with CBU-55 fuel-air-explosive (FAE) bombs to suffocate the North Vietnamese. With this, The ARVN III Corps feverishly worked on a new plan to finally link TF-15 with the An Loc garrison by deploying these new weapons and additional reinforcements. The 6th Airborne Battalion – which had been severely defeated in the Doi Gioi-Hill 169 area southeast of An Loc on 21 April – had been refurbished and was now ready to act. Its commander, Lieutenant Colonel Nguyen Van Dinh, had vowed to return to An Loc and to avenge his earlier defeat so, on 4 June, the battalion, with an effective force of 600 Paratroopers, was brought in by helicopters to FSB Long Phi, bringing with them 2,200 men as a replacement contingent for the TF-15, the 33rd Regiment and for other units. With this, the ARVN was prepared to push for An Loc and grouped themselves with the TF-15 on the left, the 33rd Regiment in the middle and the 6th Airborne Battalion on the right. At 1830 the VNAF attacked the Xa Cam entrenched positions, with the III Corps Commander, General Minh, overseeing it from his command and control helicopter. The North Vietnamese flak positions were first attacked by A-37 fighter-bombers and then by Skyraiders which dropped their parachute-enabled CBU-55 FAE canisters that vaporized and caused a series of huge explosions over an area of 1km. The 6th Airborne Battalion surged forwards and quickly overcame the North Vietnamese who offered only light and disorganized resistance. The ARVN methodically advanced from one bunker to another by throwing grenades into each hole, and as they did so, found a 300sqm bunker dug 3m down which contained 200 bodies. The North Vietnamese were killed by the pressure exerted from the CBU-55 bombs, and among the dead lay a North Vietnamese senior colonel.

The next day, the 6th Airborne Battalion continued its relentless advance and cleared out the 2km stretch of road to the Thanh Binh Hamlet in only 45 minutes, killing 73 whilst only 11 ARVN were killed and 33 wounded. Finally the link-up with An Loc was made on June 8 between the 62nd Company of the 6th Airborne Battalion, and the 81st Company of the 8th Airborne Battalion. The rest of TF-15 followed and were cheerfully met by the 1st Airborne Brigade, though during this last push into the city TF-15 had lost 153 men, with 592 wounded and 27 missing in action.

Mop-up operation

After the South Vietnamese rescuing column reached An Loc, the badly depleted North Vietnamese units pulled out, with most heading for Cambodia. However, with this loss the B2 Front leaders were determined to block any further ARVN advance north towards Loc Ninh whilst Hanoi also wished to press the South by continuing the shelling of An Loc. Ironically though, the exhausted ARVN had little reserve and the III Corps level could definitely not implement any pursuits or further actions. The national strategic reserve – constituting the Airborne and Marine Divisions – were now both committed to the I Corps for the recapture of Quang Tri, and consequently, whilst the North Vietnamese were considering their enemy's next assault moves, the South Vietnamese had few to offer and the mopping-up operations would thus drag on until the implementation of the ceasefire in January 1973. Yet as soon as the link-up took place, the An Loc garrison began to expand its occupied territory with the 81st Airborne Ranger Group and the 3rd Ranger Group, reoccupying the northern part of the city without much resistance on 10 June. Two days later the same units pushed northwards to reoccupy the Dong Long Airport and the Dong Long Hill. In the meantime, in the western sector, the 7th Regiment also retook the area fallen on 11 May during the PAVN third offensive. In the south, the 1st Airborne Brigade expanded outwards where they discovered the hulks of numerous burned out communist tanks, including a dozen T-54s abandoned inside B-52 craters, whilst approximately 3km southwest the Paratroopers found about 208 bodies with assorted weapons which highlights the devastation caused by the B-52s. In fact, by 12 June practically all areas lost within a 2km radius of An Loc were re-occupied by the South Vietnamese.

However, even if the relief column had finally broken through, Route 13 was far from clear of all roadblocks which were still proving fatal. This was highlighted on 6 June when advisor Lieutenant Colonel Edward J. Stein and the 31st Regiment were ambushed and cut off, forcing two A-37s to brave the flak and save them. Lieutenant Colonel Burr M. Willey, senior advisor to the 32nd Regiment, was not so lucky on 19 June when the same regiment, supported by 13 M41 tanks, was hit by 107mm rockets and 82mm mortars killing the entire command group. The next day, Lieutenant Colonel Charles Butler, senior advisor to the 33rd Regiment, was then subsequently killed along Route 13 and

USN A-7E VA-195, NH404 – this Corsair was attached to CVW-11 when embarked on USS *Kitty Hawk* (CVA-63) off the Vietnamese coast from February 1972 until November 1972.

VNAF F-5A, 66-9139, 522nd Fighter Squadron 23rd Tactical Wing, Bien Hoa AB – May 1972. The aircraft is armed with four BLU-27 fire-bombs (napalm).

Tom Cooper

T-54A number 312 of the PAVN 21st Armored Battalion, An Loc – June 1972. This machine formed part of one of the first batches of T-54s delivered to North Vietnam in 1964 and was still in service. Note that there are no 'smoke-evacuators' on the gun barrel, and the old wheels.

USAF O-2A, 20th TASS, Bien Hoa AB – April 1972. Note that these planes were flown by ANZAC pilots from 1972 – apparently this pilot was Australian, hence the kangaroo on its fin.

F-4D FO, 66-7555, 435th TFS/8th TFW – this is one of the few LORAN-equipped examples (shown with two variants of the SUU-13 dispenser pod family). The bigger pod is the SUU-41 – and the example is shown installed on a TER The SUU-41 was the so-called 'Gravel Pod' about which little is known. In essence, these dispensers were literal 'flying refrigerators' and were filled with liquid Freon in which various experimental weapons were then 'dipped', such as the XM40E5 Sandwich button bombs; XM44 electronic anti-intrusion devices; and even the XM48 mechanical button bomblets (gravel mines). In the lower-left corner we see a similarly-shaped, but smaller, SUU-33 CBU which was filled with anti-vehicle mines.

A PAVN BTR-50PK captured at An Loc in May 1972. A small number of these APCs had been attached to the 20th Tank Battalion and nearly all of them had been up-gunned by installing improvised turrets with ZSU-23-2 twin 23mm or ZPU-2 twin 14.5mm anti-aircraft guns on the top of the troop compartment. This vehicle had seen its heavy machine gun removed before being abandoned by its crew.

US Army AH-1G, serial 67-15836, flown by CW2 Hosaka and CW2 Henn, shot down over An Loc – 22 May 1972. It is armed with four M200 rocket launcher pods, each with 19 2.75 inch (70mm) unguided rockets.

USMC A-4F VMA-211, Bien Hoa AB – May 1972. Some 32 Skyhawks from MAG-12 were dispatched to urgently support the ARVN forces encircled inside An Loc.

VNAF A-1H, serial 135281, of the 514th Fighter Squadron from the 23rd Tactical Wing of Bien Hoa AB – May 1972. It was armed with Mk-82 HE bombs and CBU-25 dispensers.

ARVN M113, 5th Armored Cavalry Squadron – Route 13, July 1972.

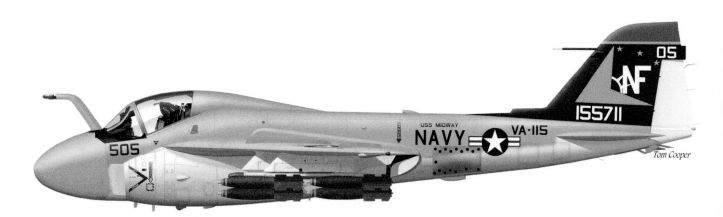

USN A-6A, NF505; VA-115 'Arabs' was deployed as part of air wing CVW-5 on board USS *Midway* (CVA-41) off Vietnam from April 1972 until March 1973. The plane is shown carrying a MER with six Mk-82 GP bombs equipped with Mk.15 Snakeye retarding fins.

VNAF CH-47A, serial 073, 237th Helicopter Squadron of the 43rd Tactical Wing, Bien Hoa AB. The Chinooks of this unit played an important role in sustaining the 'defending' troops inside An Loc.

USAF F-4D, UP 68-972, from the 35th TFS/366th TFW was one of those sent to Thailand in response to the North Vietnamese invasion in late April 1972. It is shown carrying Mk-82s with Daisy Cutter stand-off fuses and BLU-27 napalm canisters – the latter without their noses and fins.

USN A-7C, AJ410, from the VA-86 'Sidewinders' deployed on board USS *America* from June 1972 until March 1973. This carrier was usually assigned to the 1st or Atlantic Fleet of the USN but in an emergency it was sent around the world to Vietnam.

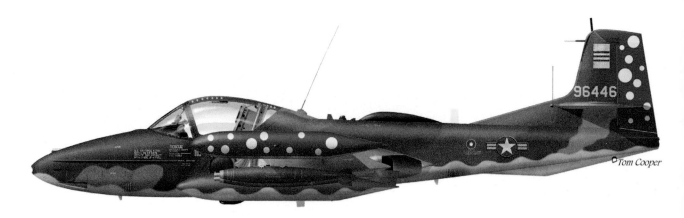

VNAF A-37B, serial 96446, 546th Fighter Squadron, 74th Tactical Wing, Binh Thuy AB. The three squadrons of this base were heavily involved in the defense of An Loc.

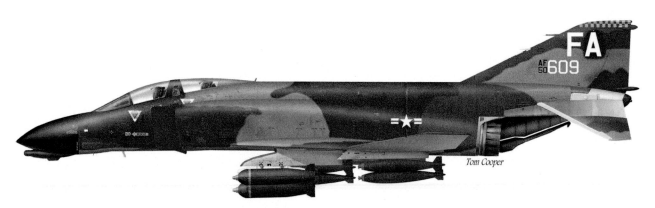

F-4D, FA 65-0609, 24th TFS/8th TFW, armed with SUU-30/B CBUs (on TER) and six Mk-82s (on TER, under the centerline), Ubon AB – Thailand, August 1972.

The T-54B, serial 377, of the PAVN 297th Armored Battalion, Dak To II FSB – 24 April 1972. This North Vietnamese tank knocked out four M41s during this battle.

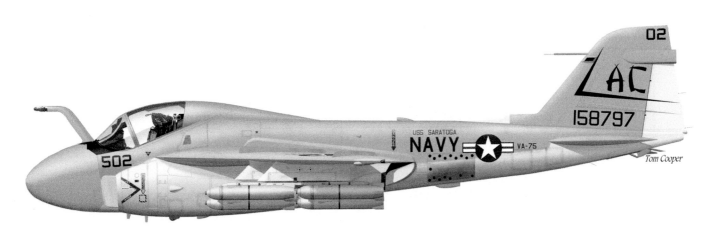

USN A-6A, VA-75, USS *Saratoga* (CV-60), August 1972. The aircraft carrier was transferred in haste from the Atlantic Fleet to South East Asia to reinforce the 7th Fleet. The aircraft was loaded with 12 Mk-20 Rockeye Cluster Bombs Each of them contained 247 anti-personnel bomblets that once released covered an approximate area of a football field.

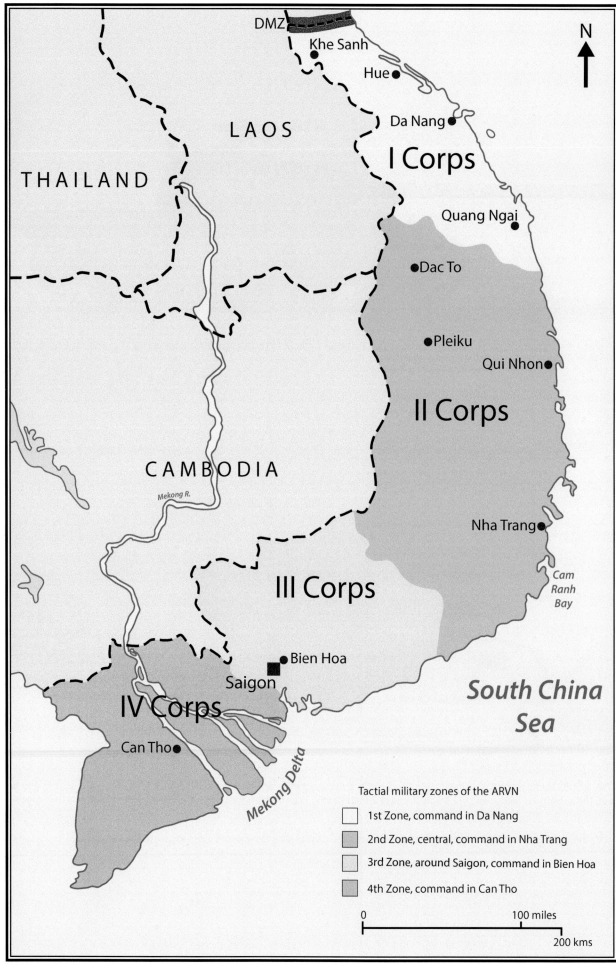

DMZ

Khe Sanh

Hue

LAOS

Da Nang

THAILAND

I Corps

Quang Ngai

●Dac To

CAMBODIA

●Pleiku

Mekong R.

Qui Nhon●

II Corps

N

Nha Trang●

Cam
Ranh
Bay

III Corps

South China
Sea

Bien Hoa

Saigon

IV Corps

Can Tho●

Mekong Delta

Tactial military zones of the ARVN

1st Zone, command in Da Nang

2nd Zone, central, command in Nha Trang

3rd Zone, around Saigon, command in Bien Hoa

4th Zone, command in Can Tho

0   100 miles

200 kms

ARVN Tactical Corps

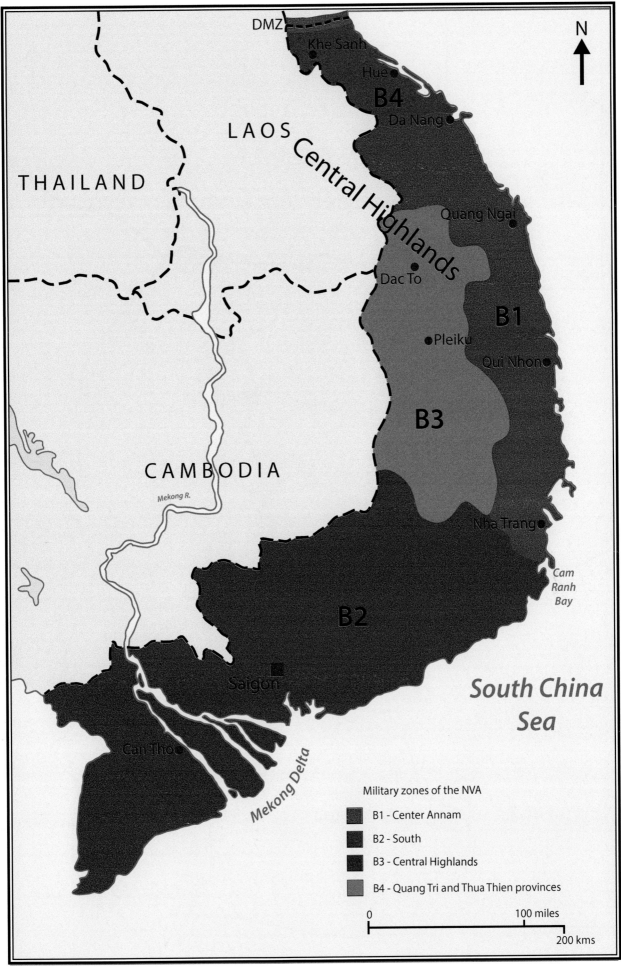

Military Zones of PAVN

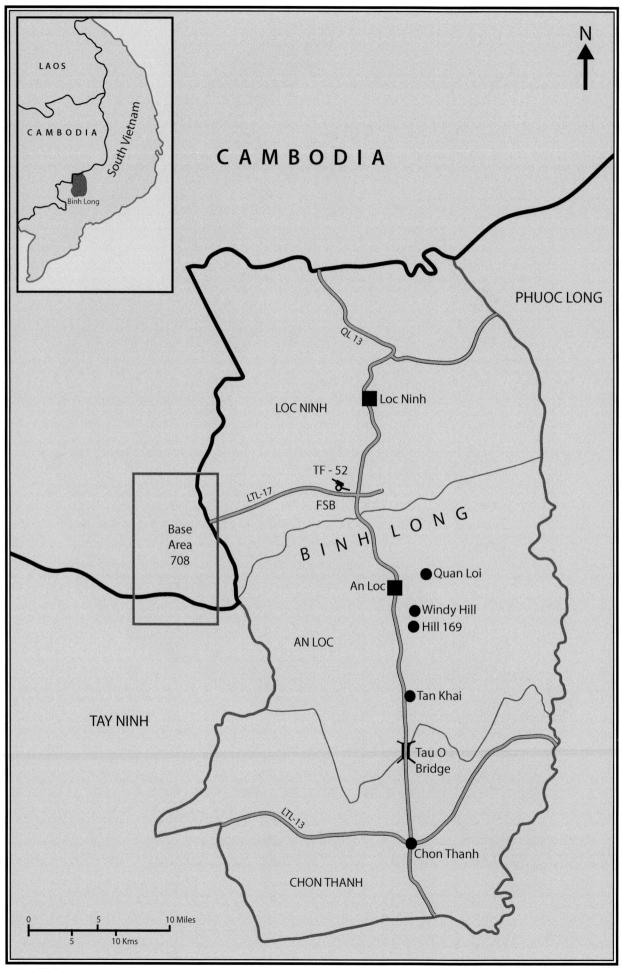

An Loc Ninh

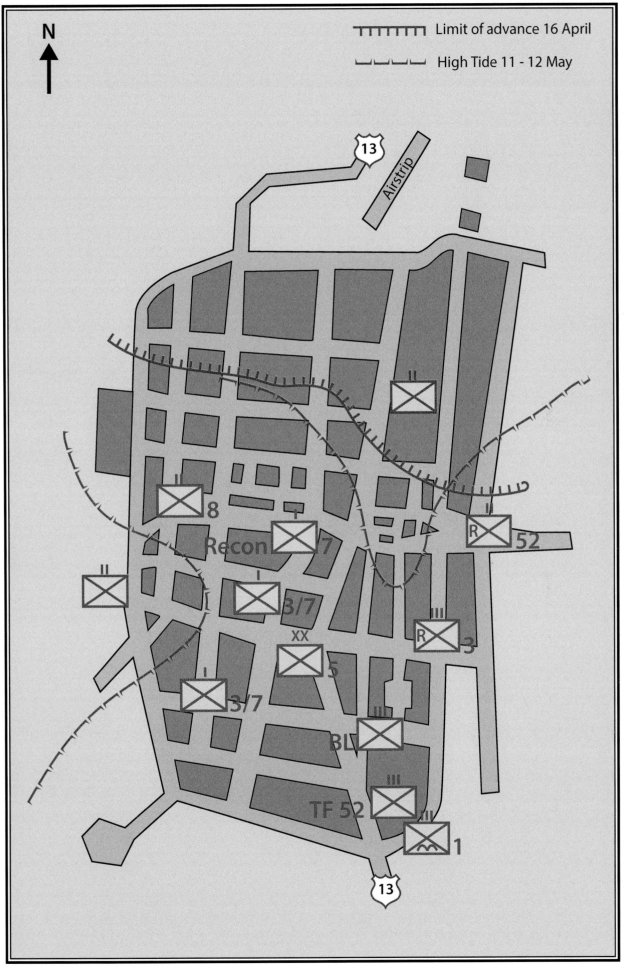

N

Limit of advance 16 April

High Tide 11 - 12 May

Siege of An Loc

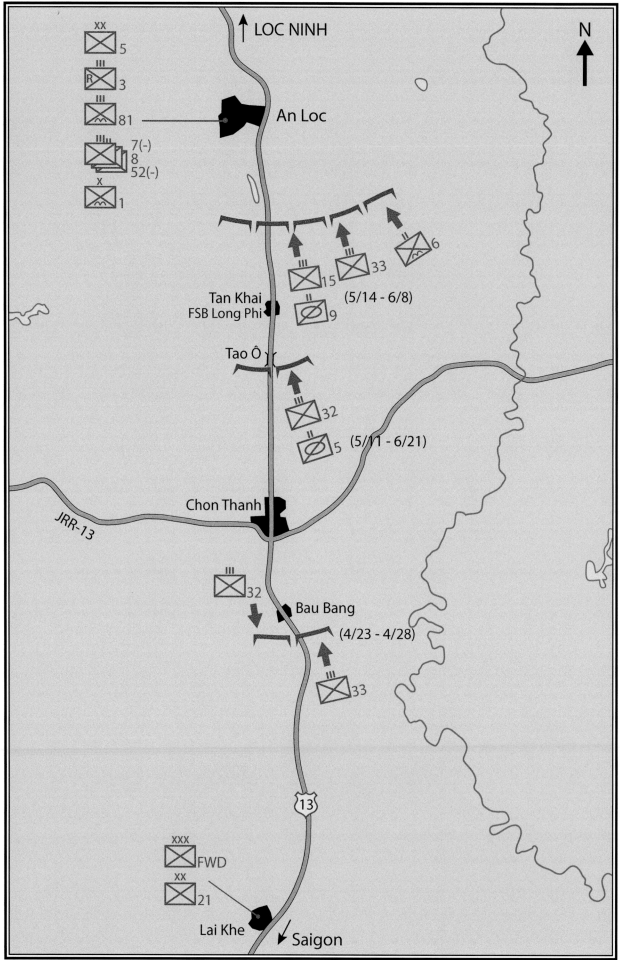

Relief Operation Route 9

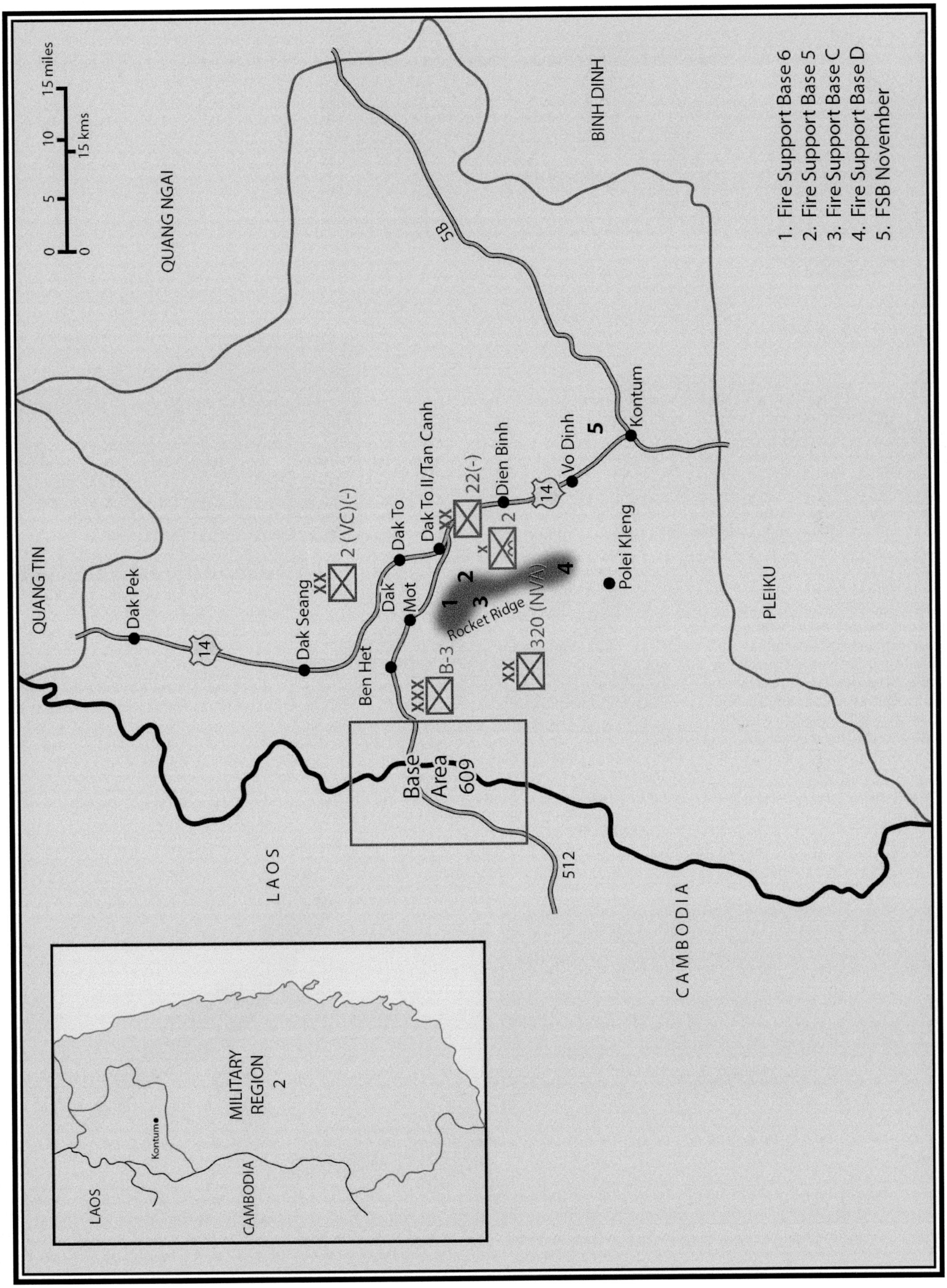

15 miles

15 kms

15

10

5

5

0

0

QUANG NGAI

BINH DINH

5B

Kontum

Vo Dinh

14

Dien Binh

5

22(-)

Dak To II/Tan Canh

x 2

Dak To

Dak Mot

XX

2

Polei Kleng

Dak Pek

Dak Seang

2 (VC)(-)

XX

14

Ben Het

Rocket Ridge

3

2

1

4

320 (NVA)

XX

PLEIKU

QUANG TIN

14

B-3

XXX

LAOS

Base Area 609

512

CAMBODIA

1. Fire Support Base 6
2. Fire Support Base 5
3. Fire Support Base C
4. Fire Support Base D
5. FSB November

MILITARY REGION 2

Kontum

LAOS

CAMBODIA

Central Highlands

A B-52D returns from an Arc Light mission at U-Tapao AB in Thailand. The Strategic Air Command made an unprecedented effort to counter the North Vietnamese offensive and deployed over 200 of its giant bombers for South East Asia operations. They mainly operated from bases in Thailand and Guam. (USAF)

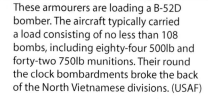

The North Vietnamese offensive prompted the USAF to rush to South East Asia additional F-4 equipped units, bringing the number of Phantoms available to 400. They were ferried across the Pacific Ocean from the United States during the Operation Constant Guard. An F-4E from the 4th TFW is being refuelled by a KC-135 during the transit flight. (USAF)

The USAF also sent in its new attack aircraft, the LTV A-7D to South East Asia by deploying the 354th TFW. The 72 Corsair IIs of the wing operated from Korat AB in Thailand. (USAF)

These armourers are loading a B-52D bomber. The aircraft typically carried a load consisting of no less than 108 bombs, including eighty-four 500lb and forty-two 750lb munitions. Their round the clock bombardments broke the back of the North Vietnamese divisions. (USAF)

The USAF began to introduce guided air munitions in significant numbers during Operation Linebacker in 1972. That included the GBU-10 Paveway laser-guided bombs such as those carried by this F-4D from the 433rd TFS of the 8th TFW of Ubon AB, Thailand. (USAF)

The F-4 Phantom was the American main fighter-bomber operating in South East Asia in 1972. In addition to those of the USAF, they were also deployed by the US Marine Corps and the US Navy. This F-4B of the VF-111 from the USS Coral Sea is seen during a bombing pass, dropping six Mk-82 500lb bombs. (US Navy)

Finally the siege of An Loc was over on 8 June 1972 when the rescuing forces linked with the forces inside the city at the southern perimeter. The Commander of the ARVN 5th Division, Colonel Le Van Hung, left, shakes hands with the Commander of the 3rd Airborne Brigade, Lieutenant Colonel Truong Vinh Phuoc, who had led the final rescue operation. (ARVN)

Every North Vietnamese bunker established along Route 13 was a tough nut to crack and required hand-to-hand fighting to overwhelm them. The South Vietnamese methodically advanced from one bunker to another by lobbing in hand grenades and satchel charges. (ARVN)

just a week later, the 33rd Regiment Commander, Lieutenant Colonel Can, was killed by enemy artillery when his unit reached Dong Phat Hamlet, southeast of An Loc. In light of all these high-profile deaths, the 1st Airborne Brigade was ordered to clear Route 13 between the city and Tan Khai where the North Vietnamese still held strong ground. The Paratroopers could also not break through however, and they were finally picked up by helicopters and taken to Saigon, Bien Hoa and Vung Tau for reorganization. Subsequently, they re-joined the rest of the Airborne Division north of Hue for the counteroffensive to retake Quang Tri in MR I. On 7 July, it was the turn of the 81st Airborne Ranger Group to leave the area after suffering heavy losses and, after a short rest, it too was sent to reinforce MR I. Its place in An Loc was taken by the 5th Ranger Group. By early July, the exhausted 21st Division was also finally returned to the Mekong Delta, where General Hau was sacked for being unable to direct during combat. The unit was replaced by the 25th Division which eventually overran the last PAVN blocking positions near Tau O on Route 13.

Now that the An Loc siege had been broken, it was decided to replace the 5th Division with the 18th Division, under the command of Colonel Le Minh Dao who was unfortunately tied down in the Binh Duong Province by the diversionary actions launched by the PAVN B2 Front. The transfer of the 18th Division into An Loc was thus delayed until 11 July when it was constituted with the 43rd, 48th and 52nd Regiments that came in addition to the 5th Ranger Group. These fresh troops continued to expand the city's perimeter and the 43rd Regiment pushed south along Route 13, overwhelming the last communist blocking position at Xa Cam. After securing its logistical line, Colonel Dao kept the 52nd Regiment and the 5th Ranger Group as reserves and sent the 48th and 43rd Regiments to recapture Doi Gio, Hill 169 and Quang Loi Airfield. The 48th Regiment attacked Hill 169 on 17 July but encountered heavy resistance, with its 3rd Battalion caught in open terrain and pounded with 82mm mortars and 75mm recoilless guns – the battalion could only withdraw thanks to VNAF A-37 air strikes – but the summit was finally taken during a night assault in the middle of a heavy rainstorm. However, during the fighting the enemy entrenched themselves on the northern crest but after 10 days of shelling this last position was also taken. The other target for the 48th Regiment – Doi Gioi Hill – was actually attacked on 9 July but only required a day's fighting to overwhelm the enemy bunkers thanks to M72 rocket launchers and hand grenades. However, despite these gains, Brigadier General Tallman, Senior

Deputy Advisor to the III Corps, was killed by a North Vietnamese artillery shell, making him the highest ranking US Army officer killed in Vietnam up to this point in the war.

Continuing, the 43rd Regiment and the 5th Ranger Group launched their attacks on 8 August against the Quang Loi Airfield. The base was protected by concrete bunkers built by the Americans and fitted with barbed wire and an outside earth wall. During the initial assault, about a third of the runway had been conquered but the well-protected enemy machine guns and mortars blocked the South Vietnamese, so the 43rd Regiment tried to envelop the southern perimeter while its 2nd Battalion attacked a hill in the west – but it suffered heavy casualties. The hill was finally taken after a night attack, and on 12 August in order to resume the advance against the last North Vietnamese-entrenched positions, the JGS sent in a TOW platoon. The concrete bunkers were then targeted by the wired-guided missiles but were finished off with M72 and XM202 rocket launchers. Major Nguyen Huu Che, commander of the 2nd Battalion, was awarded the National Order and Gallantry Cross with Palm – the highest ARVN decoration – as well as the US Silver Star for his bravery during the fighting.

In August, the 52nd Regiment expanded westwards but clashed with PAVN forces at Phu Kiem, killing 67 North Vietnamese. The 43rd Regiment was again then called to clear out a new roadblock set up by the PAVN on the route between An Loc and the Quang Loi Airfield – but with the runway now firmly in their hands, the South Vietnamese decided to pull back the 18th Division from An Loc on

29 November, with its defensive role taken over by the 3rd, 5th and 6th Ranger Groups under the command of Colonel Nguyen Thanh Chuan, when the ceasefire was proclaimed. The Battle of An Loc may definitely have been over but the casualties were massive, with ARVN sources indicating that they had lost some 2,280 troops; that 8,564 were wounded; and that 2,091 were missing in action. The North Vietnamese losses were also staggering, with an estimated 10,000 men killed and over 70 tanks destroyed.

CHAPTER 6
THE BATTLE FOR THE CENTRAL HIGHLANDS

Whilst the North Vietnamese had carried out their ruthless offensive to the great surprise of the Americans and ARVN, the expected attack against the Central Highlands had not yet materialized. In fact, contrary to allied intelligence, this area would become the last place targeted under the B3 Front commanded by Major General Hoang Minh Thao, which included the 2nd, 320A and 3rd Divisions. The latter unit was the famous 'Gold Star' Division that had operated for years in the redoubts of the Anamitic mountain chain, overlooking the Binh Dinh coastal plain. This area had only been partially pacified by the ARVN and was still a Viet Cong stronghold which even the French had failed to quash years earlier. The vital Route 1, nicknamed the 'route without joy', was also a very dangerous place for allied forces. In addition to the units listed, General Thao also had at his disposal four independent infantry regiments, two assault sapper battalions and four Viet Cong battalions. Both the 2nd and 320A Divisions had been reinforced by an artillery battalion with 120mm and 160mm heavy mortars and had also received truck transportation companies in order to bring them up to a similar standard as the motorized divisions of the central reserve in North Vietnam. Consequently, the main artillery assets were placed directly under the B3 Front control with two independent artillery regiments. These were the 675th Artillery Regiment with one battalion equipped with D-44 85mm field guns and 105mm howitzers, one battalion with 122mm howitzers and one with the redoubtable D-74 long-range 122mm guns. The 40th Artillery Regiment had three battalions equipped respectively with 105mm and 122mm howitzers; 76.2mm and 85mm guns; and 107mm and 122mm MRLs. However, the main strike force behind General Thao was the 297th Armored Battalion which was a unit that had been reinforced by a fourth company and which deployed 50 T-54 and T-34-85 tanks. There were also the 15 PT-76s of the 16th Armored Company and the 18 ZSU-57-2s of the 57th Anti-Aircraft Artillery Company. Some six Flak Battalions, equipped with towed 37mm and 57mm guns were also available, bringing the communist strength in MR II up to 50,000 troops, including 28,000 deployed in the northern Central Highlands sector.

Thus, the ARVN II Corps in charge of the Central Highlands had to contend with a huge largely uninhabited region that represented nearly 40 percent of South Vietnamese territory. Except for the coastal plain along Route 1 linking Hue and Da Nang to Saigon, most of the area was also very hilly and mountainous. The South Vietnamese MR II also contained important military bases installed in the main cities of Pleiku, Ban Me Thuout, Nha Trang, Phan Rang and Phu Cat. The Cam Ranh Bay was a modern harbor with most of the population concentrated along the coastal towns, whilst the plateau was inhabited by various tribes. The Routes 19, 7 and 21 connected the interior plateau to the coast through the An Khe and M'Drak passes which offered ideal ambush sites and chokepoints – whilst the jungle-covered mountains and valleys were ideal places for North Vietnamese infiltrations and bases. The ARVN itself could not in any way compensate the departing US Army units and could only draw on personnel within the 22nd and 23rd Divisions, three mobile Ranger Groups, 11 Border Ranger Groups, the 2nd Armored Brigade and the Regional Forces.

Adding to the volatility of this region, since February the ARVN II Corps was under the command of Lieutenant General Ngo Dzu, who was considered by many to be the worst South Vietnamese Corps Commander. General Dzu had never really exercised command of such an important job in the past, having previously served in a series of low-profile jobs at the JGS, yet he was posted to head the II Corps in August 1970 because President Thieu considered him non-political and would thus not threaten his authority. In fact, General Dzu had an over-reliance on his American senior advisor, John Paul Vann, a controversial figure who first went to Vietnam in 1962 ranked as an army Lieutenant Colonel but quickly irked his superiors by reporting in the press that the war effort was going badly, whilst denouncing a badly led counterinsurgency effort and highlighting South Vietnamese corruption. Having gone too far, he was forced to resign but managed to return to Vietnam in 1965 as an official with the Agency for International Development (USAID). Despite his outspokenness, he steadily climbed the ladder and later served as Director of Civil Operations and Revolutionary Development Support (CORDS) in ARVN IV Corps. In May 1971, in an extraordinary move, Vann was placed in charge of the US advisers in II Corps, through a combination of political patronage and recognized qualities. However, in order to select him, the military had to change its own rules with Vann now becoming 'Director' of the 'Second Regional Assistance Group' (SRAG), but his authority was no less than that of his military colleagues in I and III or IV Corps. Director Vann had in fact risen to the equivalent rank of a Lieutenant General almost a decade after shedding his army uniform. He actually lobbied for this rank – a move that would have given him three stars and made him the highest ranking Senior Corps Advisor in South Vietnam – highlighting his ego which alienated many. Several South Vietnamese officers also resented the fact that General Dzu hid behind his advisor and let him pull the strings. The 'civilian general' took risks and spent his time in the field often piloting his own helicopter amidst fierce fighting. His deputy, Brigadier General George Wear, a veteran of two Vietnam tours, was replaced by Brigadier General John Hill (himself at the end of his second Vietnam tour). Director Vann handed him control of the fire-support assets whilst he himself concentrated on directing the ARVN ground units. This conflicting command structure would seriously hinder ARVN II Corps' efficiency at critical moments in the upcoming offensive.

Due to the fact that the allied forces expected an attack in the region, the area was placed under the 22nd Division – one of the two ARVN 'heavy' divisions, with four instead of three regiments – and it was commanded by Colonel Le Duc Dat, a decision opposed by Director Vann, who wanted to choose this person himself. Therefore,

The North Vietnamese send in reinforcements to the B3 Front in the Central Highlands. These Soviet-built GAZ-52 trucks of 2.5-ton capacity ferry in the units of the 320A Division in early 1972. (PAVN)

Drivers of the PAVN 2nd Division check the status of their North Korean-built Sungri 58KA trucks of 2.5-ton capacity. Pyongyang delivered more than 2,000 of them to Hanoi for the 1972 campaign. (PAVN)

right from the start the relationship between the Director of the II SRAG and the division's commander was sour and added a new dimension to an unfolding crisis. The southern sector was held by the 23rd Division which sometimes sent units down to the coastal area if situations demanded, whilst the central coastal area between Tuy Hoa and Qui Nhon was held by two South Korean divisions on the verge of departure – but the most that could be expected from the ROK forces were security sweeps along Route 19 from Qui Nhon to An Khe.

Based on intelligence reports including the interrogations of prisoners and defectors, General Dzu and Director Vann soon decided to reinforce the defenses around the Kontum and Pleiku cities, which were the most likely PAVN targets. They decided to establish a forward defense system by creating a strong fortified position at Tan Canh and Dak To, northwest of Kontum – near the junction of Route 14, running north–south – and Route 512, going east–west. That plan was, however opposed by Director Vann's deputy, General Wear, who instead called for a series of smaller interconnected FSBs to slow down any PAVN advance. Each of these positions would then resist for as

A US Army Bell OH-58A scout helicopter flies low over a river in search of North Vietnamese infiltrations. (US Army)

long as possible and hold the North Vietnamese whilst air strikes would pummel them. Once a position was overrun, soldiers could fall back on the next and the process would be repeated, but Director Vann insisted that only a stronger fortified position could resist a North Vietnamese force equivalent to three divisions. However, in wanting a stronger position, he then did not allow General Dzu to regroup the entire 22nd Division there, instead insisting that the 40th and 41st Regiments stay in the coastal area for security task, and to quash the growing unhappiness of many at being placed under the authority of the 22nd Division commander. Despite this decision, the II Corps redeployed to protect the Central Highlands and, in phase one, the 22nd Division Headquarters was sent one infantry regiment, plus a support element and a heavy support unit. However, US scout helicopters discovered six T-54s abreast and many more east of North Vietnamese Logistic Base 609 that sat astride the Laotian border and in the Plei Trap Valley, west of the Rocket Ridge – a string of hill outposts which dominated Route 511 – forming a screen protecting Tan Canh and Kontum City from western and northwestern approaches. However, neither Director Vann nor General Dzu believed that the North Vietnamese had many tanks in the area, but it did alarm Director Vann enough to order 60 B-52 sorties against the suspected zones and the deployment of additional reinforcements; the 42nd and 47th Regiments of the 22nd Division, the division's headquarters, a substantial portion of the division's logistics and the 14th and 19th Armored Cavalry Squadrons. The 42nd Regiment,

whose reputation was one of the worst in the ARVN, as well as the division's Command Post, 22 M41s and 40 M113s, were positioned at Tan Canh, whilst the 47th Regiment was based at Dak To II, 5km to the northwest, reinforced with a troop of M113s, a troop of M41s and some old M24 tanks used as mobile pillboxes. As already indicated, the JGS had also deployed the 2nd Airborne Brigade as reinforcement and the Paratroopers were positioned on the southern portion of the Rocket Ridge, lying parallel and west of Route 14. In addition, the area around Dak To also had the Border Rangers at the bases of Ben Het, Dak Mot, Dak Pek, Dak Seang and at FSB 5 and 6. The town of Kontum and its southern approaches were further reinforced by the 1st Airborne Brigade – so all in all, the forces concentrated around Tan Canh and Dak To amounted to a reinforced division-strength force. Therefore, the overall ARVN deployment between Pleiku and Tan Canh amounted to 13 infantry battalions, including Rangers attached to the 22nd Division, six airborne battalions, and supported by 50 M41 and M24 tanks, 120 M113s and 65 howitzers. The reason behind such firepower was to block the advance of two communist divisions that had just been spotted in the vicinity of the Plei Trap Valley and the tri-borders area.

The ARVN II Corps launched probes to the west of Kontum from 15 March supported by B-52 strikes, but when Hanoi's offensive started in MR I and MR II General Dzu was extremely worried. His fears were exacerbated when the JGS withdrew the 3rd Airborne Brigade deployed south of Kontum on 20 April. It was replaced by

ARVN Border Rangers check for mines that have already damaged an M5 half-track on this trail, west of Kontum. This obsolete vehicle was employed for convoy escort operations. (ARVN)

the 6th Ranger Group from Hue whilst Director Vann also persuaded General Dzu to move the 53rd Regiment of the 23rd Division over the operational area vacated by the Paratroopers. Part of the cavalry had been redeployed west of Tan Canh to Ben Het, around 20km northwest, to block the likely approach of enemy tanks. The 1st Tank Troop of the 14th Cavalry Squadron, organic to the 22nd Division, with 15 M41s was then deployed on the important high ground

overlooking the Ho Chi Minh Trail inside Laos – where the first engagement between American and North Vietnamese tanks took place in 1969. At night from this position, troops could hear enemy trucks and Ranger patrols and subsequently reported that North Vietnamese tanks had been spotted south of Ben Het, but the ARVN M41s could not locate and engage them.

In the meantime, General Thao had accelerated the preparation

The ARVN held the 'Rocket Ridge' – a string of hill outposts which formed a screen protecting Pleiku and Kontum City from western and northwestern approaches. A Private from the 22nd Division runs to take cover from rocket fire. (US Army)

of his forces, even if the element of surprise had been lost with the opening of the Quang Tri and An Loc fronts. He intended to isolate the battlefield by sealing off the Kontum and Tan Canh area by cutting Routes 14 and 19 with the independent 12th, 28th and 95th Regiments. The 320A and 2nd Divisions, supported by the 297th Armored Battalion, would be the main striking force whilst the 3rd Division, supported by the local regular Viet Cong battalions entrenched in the mountains of the northern Binh Dinh Province, would launch diversionary attacks southeast towards the coastal plain. In a second phase after taking Tan Canh, the 320A and 2nd Divisions would move down south against Pleiku and its airbase, where the two PAVN thrusts would then join and occupy the whole Route 19, cutting South Vietnam into two isolated halves. Meanwhile, the North Vietnamese had also increased pressure on the forces screening Tan Canh and Dak To, with the 320A Division launching a series of vicious assaults against the 'Rocket Ridge' whose outposts could only be resupplied by helicopters. On 8 April, many company-sized contacts broke onto the south of the ridge leading to the events of 11 April where a barrage of 122mm artillery and rockets crashed on FSB Charlie, defended by the 11th Airborne Battalion. On 14 April the situation became even more precarious when the PAVN 48th Regiment forced the ARVN to evacuate and, as the 22nd Division tried to hold onto the ridgeline by dispatching the 1st Battalion of the 42nd Regiment, they were soon surrounded by two enemy battalions and could now not even be supplied by helicopters. Out of ammunitions, some 63 survivors out of a total of 350 troops broke out and succeeded in returning to Tan Canh.

A week later FSB Delta – on the southern end of the ridgeline – also succumbed under a heavy infantry and armor assault, led by the T-54s of the 12th Company of the 297th Armored Battalion. Now the remaining Rangers and Airborne troops in the 'Rocket Ridge' were isolated and fought for their lives but, guessing that sustaining these outposts would be too costly and fearing that the relief columns would surely be ambushed in the mountainous terrain, the 22nd Division gave up all surrounding ridgelines in the area of Dak To-Tan Canh (in the northern and eastern sectors) to the forces of the PAVN 320A Division. The North Vietnamese methodically took over the high ground positions where they quickly dug in their artillery and swiftly began shelling the 22nd Division in the valley. For two weeks Tan Canh was targeted by enemy artillery which increased up to 1,000 rounds a day but, alarmingly, the 22nd Division commander, Colonel Le Duc Dat, took no initiative to loosen the enemy encirclement and the ARVN II Corps – only relying upon increasing air strikes. Yet, despite these bombardments, the PAVN 66th Independent Regiment still managed to build a new road at over 100km long to bring supplies up to the prepared combat positions. Engineers also built caves to position artillery in the hills, set up roads to within 5km of ARVN positions, and produce ramps to be used by tanks for the assault – which were now deployed forward after traveling over 200km from their camouflaged parking areas in Laos. The T-54s of the 7th Company, the PT-76s of 16th Independent Armored Company and the ZSU-57-2s had, meanwhile, been sent to Po Co Ha, 16km east of Tan Canh, whilst the 3rd and 12th Companies were held back in reserve north of that position. Also, a part of the 2nd Company, some nine T-34-85s, and a company of towed 37mm flak was deployed at Vo Dinh in order to seal off the southwest access to Tan Canh.

On 23 April, the final blow was hammered by General Thao who set up a 2nd Division diversionary attack at the northern sector of Tan Canh whilst simultaneous attacks were carried out against the eastern side by the 66th Regiment. The rest of the 2nd Division was amassed against Dak To II Sector while the 320A Division was held back as a reserve for exploitation. He remained cautious however and feared that the South Vietnamese would launch counter-attacks with their armored assets but the ARVN had spaced out its vehicles along the barbed-wire fences, and it was decided to infiltrate using tank-killer teams armed with newly delivered AT-3s. The North Vietnamese used their wire-guided anti-tank missiles efficiently, knocking out most of the M-41s deployed at static positions around the perimeter at a distance of over 1km. Initially the South Vietnamese tank crews were stunned and many abandoned their vehicles but, needing to take charge of the situation, American advisors ordered the surviving M41s to move out and thus make harder targets of themselves. Meanwhile a number of bunkers were also destroyed by the AT-3 launching teams and at 1030 the division's Command Post was hit by several missiles that destroyed nearly all the communication equipment, killing or wounding over 20 men. Without control and coordination, the ARVN units were left to fend for themselves whilst the advisors tried their best to help, directing air support with regimental communication assets. Director Vann then met Colonel Dat who had promised B-52 strikes, but the situation was becoming so desperate that Director Vann soon ordered American advisors be readied to implement an escape plan; it seems that he had not tried to replace the destroyed communication center to re-establish the 22nd Division Command Post but, instead, bluntly told Colonel Dat that he would be the first ARVN Division Commander to lose his division. Director Vann took off by helicopter at 1200 with some advisors shortly before another artillery barrage was unleashed on the base, followed by several probes on the eastern perimeter. Throughout that evening the 42nd

Regiment held its ground against several assaults carried out by the 2nd Division, but when darkness fell enemy attacks increased whilst most of the air support had ceased.

In the meantime, the PAVN 7th Armored Company had tried to launch a diversionary attack against the eastern perimeter of Tan Canh but its move had been detected and the tanks came under artillery fire at a crossing on the Dac Ta Cam River. The South Vietnamese called in air support but it took two hours before the arrival of an AC-130H gunship, Spectre 11, flown by Captain Russel T. Olson. He promptly attacked the column of 18 T-54s but could not stop them all, making a fast turnaround to rearm and refuel at Pleiku (a VNAF AC-47 fell in to support), but aside from these two aircraft the 22nd Division received no other fire support. At daybreak when Captain Olson was forced to leave (after claiming seven tanks) the tank commander deployed at Ben Het took the initiative to return to reinforce the soldiers of Tan Canh himself. But this hastily planned move, using Route 512 through hills and jungles, led the two armored troops and infantry platoon into an ambush led by a large PAVN force of the 320A Division, and nine of the 12 M-41 tanks and other vehicles were subsequently destroyed.

After being constantly pounded by night air attacks, 7th Company

Commander, Captain Bui Dinh Dot, decided to drive down Route 18 where he was joined by infantry-mounted trucks to a bridge leading into the eastern entry gate of Tan Canh. Despite it being defended by several blockhouses and a 106mm recoilless gun, the communist tanks units were shocked that the ARVN soldiers had actually been able to get through, so they broke rank and fled through the defense perimeter. Through binoculars, Captain Dot could now see that the Tan Canh defensive positions were being pummelled and he therefore gave the order to wait for the rest of the 297th Armored Battalion and the ZSU-57-2s before attacking. When the artillery barrage lifted, the stunned South Vietnamese discovered that the enemy sappers had already made it to the point of working on the barbed wires and minefields in order to clear safe pathways for the T-54s of the 7th Company. They drove through it with the 66th Infantry Regiment, whilst the 1st Platoon went directly to the 22nd Division Command Post but encountered fierce resistance, with three T-54s being knocked out by M72s – but the tanks advanced among the trenches and blockhouses, methodically destroying them. With this, tank number 352 finally reached the Command Post and fired into it at point blank range where the body of Colonel Le Duc Dat was soon

The American II Corps senior advisor was a civilian – Director John Paul Vann – a one-off in the Vietnam War. He was also Director of the Second Regional Assistance Group (SRAG), and is seen here posing with his staff. (US Army)

Tracked-tractor drivers who belong to the PAVN 675th Artillery Regiment are issued orders by an officer. The front movers are a mix of most models in service at that point with the North Vietnamese, including three ATS-59s, an AT-S and an AT-L5. (PAVN)

A US Army Bell AH-1G Cobra from 361st Aerial Weapons Company of the 17th Combat Aviation Group takes off for another attack sortie in support of troops in the ARVN 22nd Division. (US Army)

The PAVN 297th Armored Battalion of the B3 Front had only three engineering armored vehicles, which included a T-54 tank fitted with a PT-54 mine-clearing roller-device and two MTU-12 bridge layer tanks. One of these vehicles is seen deploying its 12m single-span bridge. (PAVN)

found. The deputy division commander, Colonel Vi Van Binh, and some of his staff were also taken prisoner. Other fighting took place around the Command Post of the 42nd Regiment where the T-54s destroyed four M41s, whilst other tanks went to the northern entry and attacked from the rear, opening the way for the rest of the T-54s and PT-76s that drove down Route 14. One PT-76 was then destroyed by an M41 in ambush but the other PT-76s immediately engaged the four M41s and the two M113s deployed near the ammunition dump. With all this raging, confusion amongst the South Vietnamese reached a climax when they were attacked on the southern perimeter

by the T-34-85s of the 2nd Company – and by noon, practically all ARVN resistance had ceased inside Tan Canh Base. Stragglers from the 42nd Regiment who had tried to flee south were caught en masse in a net move established by the PAVN 28th Regiment whilst many others were killed in the pursuit.

In the meantime, the North Vietnamese had also attacked the Dak To II positions and its landing strip, even though the base had been considerably reinforced with artillery during the previous weeks. The initial assault was carried out by the 2nd Division at daybreak and the North Vietnamese soon penetrated the defense lines in the northeast sector, supported by the 15 T-54s of the 3rd Company of

Once the bridge was in place, it was used by a group of T-34-85 tanks to cross over a small stream. Even if the 297th Armored Battalion mostly used the T-54 tanks, it still had a company operating the older T-34-85. (PAVN)

In addition to the organic artillery battalions attached to each North Vietnamese division operating in the Central Highlands, the B3 Front also deployed a battalion of 122mm howitzers of the 40th Artillery Regiment. (PAVN)

The North Vietnamese forces in the Central Highlands were reinforced by six anti-aircraft battalions equipped with 37mm and 57mm guns. (PAVN)

Under direct command of the B3 Front was a battalion of D-74 122mm guns of the 675th Artillery Regiment. However, they were no match in terms of range or precision to the ARVN weapons in the Central Highlands. (PAVN)

A battery of ZPU-1 14.5mm heavy anti-aircraft machine guns of the PAVN 2nd Division is being positioned atop a hill awaiting camouflage. (PAVN)

the 297th Armored Battalion. At the same time, a North Vietnamese battalion and a platoon of T-54s attacked the northwest perimeter – and within an hour a fleeing US Army UH-1H helicopter with six American advisors on board was shot down by anti-aircraft fire. Indeed, throughout the day Cobras tried to cover rescue attempts by OH-58s, with Director Vann himself making eight trips, even though

his OH-58 was hit on his first of four trips. On his last rescue mission, his small liaison helicopter was assaulted by 15 to 20 panicked ARVN soldiers while it was taking off. The overloaded machine hit the ground and was damaged, injuring its crew, including Director Vann. Yet, as the battle developed it was becoming clear that the 47th Regiment offered stiffer resistance than at Tan Canh and the communist tanks were soon forced to disperse under several air attacks. Some aircraft dropped CS gas canisters, usually used to 'sanitize' a whole area in covering a rescue aerial operation but the crews of the T-54s just closed their hatches and, thanks to the overpressure created by their NBC system, were not affected by the paralyzing air. However, it was only by early evening that a successful penetration was achieved by the 1st Regiment of the 2nd Division. The North Vietnamese progressed towards the regimental Command Post but several T-54s were damaged by M72 firing. Two M41s then surged forwards and fired three rounds each against the leading T-54 but to no avail: the South Vietnamese crews had run out of anti-tank shells and whilst smoke billowed from the North Vietnamese tank it ran again and fired two quick-succession rounds on the first M41, which exploded, before it finished off the remaining Walker Bulldog with a single round.

A platoon of ARVN tanks did, however, still resist in the runway sector, shielding behind earth parapets but here too the T-54s of the 7th Company soon overwhelmed them. The leading North Vietnamese tank number 377 surprised the South Vietnamese tankers and quickly

The M41A3s of a tank troop belonging to the 19th ACS move out of Kontum to be redeployed to Tan Canh near the ARVN 22nd Division advanced Command Post. Note the sandbags installed around the turrets for additional protection against the RPG shaped-charge rockets. (US Army)

The PAVN 297th Armored Battalion are reinforced with a fourth company equipped with T34-85 tanks for the Central Highlands campaign. They are in addition to the T-54s that were clearly superior to the ARVN M24s and M41s. (PAVN)

Most of the ARVN tanks were concentrated northwest of Kontum, in the Tan Canh-Dak To II area, at the junction of Routes 14 and 512. However, instead of being used in an offensive they were kept for protecting the artillery of the 22nd Division. (Albert Grandolini Collection)

destroyed four M41s and the T-54 that followed it destroyed two other M41s and a single M24. By the end of the day all resistance, which amounted to a full ARVN division-strength force, was silenced and the North Vietnamese prowled the battlefield, towing away twenty-four 105mm and four 155mm artillery pieces, whilst four M41s and five M113s were found intact and pressed into service. In fact, the ARVN losses amounted to the equivalent of a division in the Tan Canh and Dak To II area, with 54 artillery pieces and 30 tanks taken. Due to this, the USAF and the VNAF started destroying equipment and during one of these missions an OV-10 FAC called in a flight of F-4s armed with the new 2,000lb laser-guided bombs and took out three guns and five trucks. The experimental 1st Combat Aerial TOW Team was then employed on 2 May with the NUH-1B gunships destroying four M41s, a 105mm howitzer and a 2.5-ton truck abandoned at FSB Lam Son.

In the meantime, the exposed positions of Polei Kleng, FSB Lam Son and November, as well as Ben Het, situated north and northwest of Kontum, were isolated and heavily shelled from 24 April–5 May, prompting the evacuation of most of their US advisors. The North Vietnamese wanted to eliminate these threats, so on 9 May Polei Kleng was attacked by the PAVN 64th Regiment, supported by 20 tanks, forcing the 62nd Border Ranger Battalion to evacuate, but not before

destroying five T-54s with their M72s. In Ben Het the garrisoned 71st and 95th Border Ranger Battalions were also under heavy attack and the base was severely hit by 122mm guns and 160mm heavy mortars which destroyed five 105mm and two 155mm howitzers. Also on 9 May, a battalion of the 66th Regiment attacked with their tank support and two PT-76s were destroyed at the main gate by an AC-130, while two more were destroyed by the M72s in the eastern sector. The 16th Armored Company then sent an additional platoon of tanks but three more PT-76s were destroyed by the NUH-1B TOW-armed helicopters. Constantly supported by air units, Ben Het managed to resist enemy assaults until the fall whilst the 320A Division continued its pressure on the 'Rocket Ridge', but FSB Delta fell on 21 April after being attacked by a platoon of T-54s. On 25 April the II Corps decided to evacuate the last outposts, ordering the Rangers to extricate themselves from FSBs 5 and 6. Immediately exploiting this decision, the PAVN attacked FSB Dien Binh, wiped out two regional battalions and captured six 105mm howitzers and two AH-1G Cobra helicopters. With this last protective screen removed, Kontum City, 50km south of Tan Canh, was now exposed to the enemy.

While the North Vietnamese were gaining ground around Tan

The tanks of the PAVN 297th Armored Battalion spearhead the assault against the Dak To II base. This includes the T-54s and T-34-85s which claim several South Vietnamese tanks. This poor quality but rare photo shows one ARVN M24 and one M41 destroyed in a quick fight by a T-54. Another T-54 also destroyed no less than four Walker Bulldogs. (PAVN)

As the ARVN tanks remained static inside the Tan Canh base, the AT-3 Sagger teams could pick them off one by one. They destroyed over 30 M41s and M113s in what was the most successful anti-tank missile engagement of the entire war. One of their victims was this M41A3 from 1/19th Armored Cavalry Squadron. (PAVN)

North Vietnamese troops of the 2nd Division overwhelm the Dak To II base, 5km northwest of Tan Canh, on 24 April 1972. They went on to capture this M41A3 that seems to still be intact. (PAVN)

North Vietnamese troops deployed the 9M14 Malyutka (NATO codenamed AT-3 Sagger) ATGM missiles for the first time when they attacked the Tan Canh base on 23 April 1972. (PAVN)

Canh and Dak To, the PAVN 3rd Division also attacked Binh Dinh and cut off Route 1 at the Bong Son Pass and isolated northern districts of Hoai An, Hoai Nhon and Tam Quan. This forced the 40th Regiment of the 22nd Division – deployed on the coastal area – to abandon its two major bases, FSB English and FSB Orange. The North Vietnamese now pushed rapidly northwards along Route 1 and southwest along the Kim Son River, crushing all ARVN forces in the area. The three northern districts of Binh Ding Province were now also lost and the narrow coastal lowland of the country was practically cut in two. At the same time, the 3rd Division dispatched its 12th Regiment to cut the vital Route 19 between the Mang Yang and An Khe Passes, linking Qui Nhon on the coast to Pleiku. Supported by six T-34-85s of the 2nd Company of the 297th Armored Battalion, two infantry battalions which entrenched on the hills cut the route to all traffic. It took two weeks for elements of the South Korean 9th Division and the ARVN 44th Regiment of the 23rd Division to reopen that vital logistic artery, with the first attempt on 17 April – led by a troop of 10 M41s – being easily repelled. The next day, the South Koreans charged uphill but could not advance far due to crisscrossing machine gun fire and the North Vietnamese also lowered their 23mm and 37mm guns of the 200th Anti-Aircraft Battalion for additional firepower. The USAF then mobilized four C-130s, each fitted with large rubber fuel bladders in the cargo compartments, to bring in supplies and

In a single stroke, the North Vietnamese opening phase on the Central Highlands eliminated the equivalent of a reinforced ARVN division in only two days. They captured many types of equipment, including this M42 Duster. (PAVN)

The North Vietnamese 2nd Division occupied FSB Dien Binh, north of Kontum, on 26 April, where they captured these two US Army Bell AH-1G Cobras: why they had been caught on the ground remains unknown. (PAVN)

reinforcements because trucks could not pass. The bladders also permitted the delivery of 4,500 gallons of fuel per sortie which were emptied via pumps within 15 minutes. They were joined in their efforts by normal cargo C-130s and even C-141s which brought in munitions and troops, and flew out civilians. On one of these flights a C-141A took off with a record 394 passengers – the most ever lifted by a Starlifter and more than four times the normal load. After nine more days of bloody stalemate, the South Koreans launched the final assault against Hill 638 supported by ARVN M41s and their own M113s and M132 flamethrower vehicles. The North Vietnamese subsequently

withdrew but the cost of reopening Route 19 was heavy, with the South Koreans losing 110 troops and 384 wounded, whilst 705 North Vietnamese were also killed. However, over the previous days, the North Vietnamese had isolated the battlefield by cutting Route 14 at the Chu Pao Pass – nicknamed the 'Rock Pile' – between Pleiku and Kontum, 10km south of the latter city. The 95B Regiment, entrenched with anti-aircraft guns, had withstood several ARVN advances, meaning that Kontum City was only sustained by an air bridge and the PAVN was now preparing to attack it.

CHAPTER 7
THE SIEGE OF KONTUM

The ARVN forces in northwestern MR II were in complete meltdown with the fall of Tan Canh and, worse still, it seemed only a matter of time before Kontum would also topple. To stop this, it was initially envisaged to carpet-bomb the abandoned positions along the 'Rocket Ridge' with the B-52s but because of the thousands of fleeing refugees, escaping 22nd Division soldiers and, many American advisors still missing, the scheme was scrubbed. Instead, more precise tactical air strikes mostly flown by the VNAF were ordered between 24–26 April,

with some 180 sorties eventually being carried out.

With their massive failures on the battleground, the now demoralized survivors of the 22nd Division could only offer token resistance and most were in fact sent to the Binh Dinh Province for refitting and training. Out of necessity a new division commander, Colonel Pham Dinh Niem, was appointed: a competent and aggressive leader he would steadily rebuild the tarnished reputation of the unit, and his first move was to reshuffle a shaken ARVN command structure. Lieutenant General Ngo Dzu, after the disaster at Tan Can,

The PAVN 3rd Division cut this vital Route 19 between the Mang Yang and An Khe Passes, linking the Central Highlands to the coast. This ARVN logistic convoy was destroyed when trying to pass through the An Khe Pass. (ROK Army)

The task of reopening Route 19 fell to the ROK 9th Division from Qui Nhon on the coast. The South Korean 'Tiger' Division used its own M113s, supported by ARVN M41 tanks. (ROK Army)

It took the ROK 9th Division more than two weeks of heavy fighting to clear the blockade and reopen the An Khe Pass. The logistic convoys soon resumed their journeys to Pleiku. (ROK Army)

The demoralized ARVN 40th Regiment of the 22nd Division evacuate its position in the northern Binh Dinh Province at the approach of the North Vietnamese 3rd Division which practically spread to the sea, severing the strategic coastal Route 1. Under the watch of a V100 armored car, a convoy made up of M35 and Toyota DW 15L trucks head south, having abandoned FSB English. (Albert Grandolini Collection)

M41A3s from the 18th ACS, attached to the 23rd ARVN Division that had taken over the defense of Kontum, ran aggressive sweeps as they waited for the enemy offensive. (ARVN)

Toan, the former commander of the ARVN Armor Branch, succeeded in raising troops' morale, but he clashed with Director Vann who did not like having a 'free-thinker'.

The 2nd and 6th Ranger Groups were charged with delaying the North Vietnamese push southwards but they were eventually replaced by the two still uncommitted regiments of the 23rd Division. This decision was made because the Rangers were both exhausted and needed elsewhere on more threatened Fronts, whilst the nature of the ARVN as well as II Corps command systems also meant that the command for upcoming battles would be placed in the hands of the commander of the 23rd Division, Colonel Ly Tong Ba. However, his authority was challenged by both the Rangers and Paratroopers, as well the regional troops who had their own command channels: therefore, again the nature of the South Vietnamese military made any inter-service cooperation a challenging task. The fact that Colonel Ba also held the same rank as many of the officers placed under his command also created additional difficulties, and he was not highly regarded by Director Vann himself, their feud stemming back to 1963.

The rest of the 23rd Division was moved out of Ban Me Thout, some 160km south, leaving the defense of southern MR II to Regional Forces alone. By deploying the entire 23rd Division into Kontum, the 44th and 45th Regiments replaced two Ranger Groups and an airborne brigade, which came in addition to the 53rd Regiment already in place. Part of the deployment was made by air due to the fact that on the last leg of the trip, the North Vietnamese had cut Route 14 south of Kontum at the Chu Pao Pass. The troops were flown in by the USAF C-130Es and the VNAF C-123Ks while the artillery was hauled by Chinook helicopters. Colonel Ba accelerated the preparation of the defense of Kontum and was helped by his new senior advisor, Colonel Rhotenberry, with whom he had developed a better working relationship than with his former American counterpart. He positioned the 44th Regiment astride Route 41, about 4km northwest of the town and, supported by the 45th Regiment which held the northern sector, the 53rd Regiment was deployed on the northeastern side, protecting the airfield. Two battalions of the Territorial Forces were also assigned

was unable to exercise his functions and sank into a deep depression where he would incessantly call President Thieu and plead for advice, even on the most menial things. President Thieu replaced him with Major General Nguyen Van Toan who was serving as the Assistant of Operations in MR I. However, during this time General Toan was being investigated by the South Vietnamese Anti-Corruption Inspectorate. Yet, known to be as one of the few ARVN officers capable of commanding an important mechanized combined force, President Thieu promoted him to take over the II Corps on 10 May. General

Kontum was surrounded and held by only an air bridge that was occasionally interrupted due to enemy artillery fire directed against the local airbase. The three VNAF squadrons of C123K Providers played a crucial role in sustaining the encircled garrison, bringing in supplies and ammunition, and flying out the wounded and civilians. (Albert Grandolini Collection)

One of the two NUH-1B helicopters from the 1st Combat Aerial TOW Team which is deployed to Kontum to test the new wire-guided anti-tank missile. The unit claimed a total of 47 kills, including 24 tanks. (US Army)

A group of T-34-85s of the PAVN 297th Armored Battalion support another assault against Kontum in May 1972. These obsolete tanks were still useful in support roles and could deal quite successfully with the ARVN M41s. (PAVN)

This T-54B was destroyed via M72 LAW rockets by the ARVN 44th Regiment near FBS November. (ARVN)

A group of T-54Bs attack the northern perimeter of Kontum but, just as they did at An Loc, the North Vietnamese performed poorly, spreading their assets thinly instead of bringing them together in stronger formations. (PAVN)

to the defense of the southern and southeastern approaches and were made up of some 2,500 tribesmen who had fled the North Vietnamese advance with their families and were issued M1 carbines. With this strengthening, the Kontum garrison totaled 11 battalions, forty-four 105mm and four 155mm howitzers as well as 18 M41 tanks. There was

also a very secret US Army combat unit which was an experimental team from the 82nd Airborne Division, equipped with TOW anti-tank missiles mounted on eight M151 Jeeps, with 10 other vehicles held at Pleiku in addition to another US Army team charged with testing the airborne version of the TOW mounted on NUH-1B helicopters and based at Pleiku. Colonel Ba would regularly visit and raise morale amongst his troops, rehearse counter-attack and artillery plans, and he also insisted that all the units be given the opportunity to practise firing the M72 LAW. Photos of destroyed T-54s at An Loc and Quang

A T-54B destroyed by a NUH-1B TOW-equipped gunship helicopter outside the Kontum perimeter. (Hughes International)

T-54s of the PAVN 297th Armored Battalion operate in the area of Kontum. (PAVN)

Between each main attack carried out against Kontum, the North Vietnamese constantly harassed the 'defenders' of the besieged city with artillery and direct tank-fire. Here, a PT-76B from the 16th Independent Armored Company – attached to the 297th Armored Battalion – opens fire from a prepared position. (PAVN)

A North Vietnamese T-54B supports a night assault against the sector held by the ARVN 44th Regiment, near FSB November. (PAVN)

Tri were also shown to the troops in order to boost confidence.

However, whilst the ARVN was expecting the next ruthless North Vietnamese offensive the PAVN B3 Front seemed unable to exploit its success at Tan Canh, and it became bogged down. In fact, just like after their victory at Dong Ha in MR I or Loc Ninh in MR III, the communists were surprised by the quick collapse of their enemy and could not move away from their 'assault timetable'. During all the

PAVN training – as well as in their doctrine of use – the emphasis was always on respecting and sticking to plans and schedules. Furthermore, their lack of experience in mechanized operations precluded any daring schemes and ground-level decisions were not generally taken. It actually took them 15 days before resuming their advance down south of Route 14. Despite heavy shelling, their tanks and artillery units were ready for a night attack but, on 12 May, an OH-6 scout discovered a group of camouflaged tanks near Vo Dinh and, in a unique duel, one of the T-54s fired against the helicopter with its 100mm gun, bringing it down. Several flights of Phantoms were later dispatched against the suspected area and claimed one of the tanks but by the second week of May, the PAVN 320A Division was positioned north of Kontum, while the 2nd Division was deployed on an arc, from northeastern to southern sectors. In order to further isolate the city, the North Vietnamese began shelling the city's airport which initially only took the form of rocket-fire, but on 11 May the situation became too dangerous so the USAF shifted to night landings only. The USAF ground control team used Ground Control Approach (GCA) radar to guide the Hercules with all lights off: then, just before the C-130 touched the ground, the pilot switched the landing lights on, and as it rolled down the runway the pallets rolled off the lowered ramp door at the rear of the aircraft, meaning that the cargo plane was only on the ground for a matter of minutes.

Having encircled Kontum, General Thao now planned the next phase which would stun the ARVN in a sudden tank-infantry assault after a brief 20-minute artillery onslaught. The offensive began on 14 May by simultaneous attacks across the entire ARVN enclave. The northwest sector was attacked by the 48th and 64th Regiments of the 320A Division, along Route 14. The 48th Regiment was deployed against the ARVN 44th Regiment, which held FSB November, whilst the 64th Regiment attacked from north-northwest on the east side of the Route 14, hitting the ARVN 45th Regiment. The 53rd Regiment on the eastern perimeter was then attacked by the 28th Regiment of the B3 Front and, finally, the southern sector was attacked by the 141st Regiment of the 2nd Division that also launched diversionary attacks against the airport sector with its 1st Regiment. However, thanks to intelligence warnings, notably SIGINT intercepts, the ARVN defenders were not caught lacking. Furthermore, contrary to the attacks carried out against Tan Canh and Dak To II – where the

Soldiers from the ARVN 23rd Division counter-attack to regain lost ground from a new penetration at the Kontum defense perimeter. (ARVN)

In addition to the NUH-1B gunship helicopters, there was also an experimental team from the 82nd Airborne Division that was equipped with TOW anti-tank missiles mounted on M151 Jeeps inside Kontum. This secret detachment was probably the last US Army ground unit to be engaged in Vietnam. (USAF)

The ARVN effectively used the artillery at its disposal inside the Kontum perimeter, where nearly 50 howitzers were available. Here a battery of 105mm pound communist positions. (ARVN)

Two soldiers of the ARVN 23rd Division inspect a destroyed North Vietnamese truck at Kontum. They are armed with M16 rifles and an M79 grenade launcher. (ARVN)

PAVN units operated closely between tanks and infantry – here that cooperation was botched. One reason for this could be that the North Vietnamese had expected long-drawn battles and consequently had felt the need to disperse their armor within companies and platoons. For that first assault they only engaged 20 T-54s and kept the others in reserve. When the attack commenced at dawn on 14 May, the North Vietnamese approach routes were quickly detected and hit by ARVN artillery, and along Route 14 a column of 10 tanks was spotted reaching the exposed FSB November. Initially the defenders of the 44th Regiment were supported by an AC-130 but that was soon forced to depart to refuel and to rearm, but by now the North Vietnamese tanks soon found themselves advancing alone because their accompanying infantry had been killed by the shelling. With this, the ARVN tank-killer teams went into action with their M72s, XM202s and captured RPGs. A first group of five T-54s of the 2nd Company of the 297th Tank Battalion pressed on but the leading tank was destroyed at close range by a South Vietnamese soldier firing his quadruple XM202 tube, the next was dispatched by the firing of an M72, whilst the third was destroyed by a mine. Seeing that their progress along the main entry of FSB November was compromised, the seven remaining tanks tried to bypass it by driving up a small stream but were themselves engaged by the NUH-1B TOW-equipped helicopters that destroyed two of them. The rest fled but returned to attack the ARVN positions that evening, where a T-54 was soon destroyed by a TOW fired from an M151 vehicle. Despite persistent assaults, most of the North Vietnamese penetrations had been repelled and most of the remaining tanks pulled back but the retreating PAVN tanks were picked off by the TOW missiles.

The PAVN renewed its assaults at night, focusing its effort on the 44th and 53rd Regiments making the situation at FSB November so critical that its commander was nearly forced to call in friendly artillery to pound its own positions to kill the North Vietnamese infantry. Luckily at the last moment an AC-130 was redirected to support the hard-pressed regiment but in the confusion of close-quarter night fighting, a North Vietnamese battalion managed to break through a gap between the two regiments and as the hours passed it was supported by tanks. Colonel Ba then took the decision to pull back the 53rd Regiment whilst under cover from two B-52-diverted strikes. This bold and risky move would take place a few times as the withdrawal of troops went to schedule, rocking the town and the PAVN. At dawn, the ARVN counter-attacked and counted over 400 enemy bodies and 18 tanks destroyed, including seven by the TOW missiles. Kontum was, for a very short period of time, saved.

While reorganizing their forces over 10 days, the North Vietnamese now pummelled the town with artillery and continuously launched probes against the external ARVN positions – with the most targeted area being the airfield sector. Due to the heavy artillery munitions expenditure, the USAF reverted back to daylight operations in order to replenish stocks but a North Vietnamese sapper team infiltrated at night and ignited 150,000 gallons of JP-4 aviation fuel and forced the American aviators to resume night operations. The VNAF persisted on day operations despite the risks and two more C-123Ks were destroyed on 15 May. That same night, a group of six T-34-85s were seen advancing against the northern perimeter and attacked by an AC-130 with its 40mm guns. The damaged tanks pressed forward nevertheless and, from prepared hull-down positions, harassed the ARVN positions, covering the infiltration of sappers. At least one tank was destroyed by a TOW missile fired by an UH-1B which attacked under night-flares dropped by the AC-130. The following evening, the same scenario unfolded but this time a group of T-54s fired on the airport with their 100mm guns. The American TOW-armed M151 Jeeps toured the sector trying to locate the hiding tanks, and whilst five were detected they were outside its range and only a single T-54 was destroyed. The following night, some seven T-54s harassed the positions held by the 44th Regiment but one hit a mine and three were destroyed by air support, whilst the three remaining tanks were found abandoned with their engines still running. Seventeen night C-130 deliveries on 19 May, and 15 more on the 20 May, sustained the flow of supplies. However, another VNAF C-123K was destroyed by rockets and three helicopters damaged. Communist sappers also infiltrated inside the southern sector held by the RF troops, while artillery spotters were discovered disguised as civilian refugees.

Due to the incessant pressure, Colonel Ba decided to rearrange ARVN deployment, pulling forces back further towards the town in order to tighten the perimeter. He then switched positions among the deployed regiments to add more depth by moving the 44th Regiment back into a reserve position and replacing it with the 45th Regiment. On 20 May, a North Vietnamese probe opened a new salient between them and the 53rd Regiment, but a determined counter-attack led by nine M-41 tanks regained the lost ground. That night, the PAVN 406th Sapper Battalion cut Route 14, 3km northwest of Kontum City and at the same time an additional North Vietnamese battalion penetrated between the defensive lines of the 4th Battalion of the 45th Regiment and the 2nd Battalion of the 53rd Regiment. An immediate counter-

This North Vietnamese T-54 was found abandoned at the end of May 1972 on the northern sector of Kontum. The ARVN sent in an M548 tracked tractor to try and tow it back. (US Army)

ARVN soldiers bring back this DshK 12.7mm anti-aircraft heavy machine gun to Kontum. (ARVN)

attack was ordered by the 3rd and 4th Battalions of the 44th Regiment and the 1st Battalion of the 45th Regiment, and the lost ground was retaken after heavy fighting. A series of limited counter-attacks were then launched by elements of the 45th and 53rd Regiments that landed by helicopter at LZ between 4–8km north of the city. Colonel Ba, along with Director Vann, regularly visited the frontlines to direct units and raise morale during these dark days.

The second assault against Kontum

As the first rains of the monsoon season fell and logistical re-supplying became increasingly difficult, it was now only a matter of 'when' the North Vietnamese would launch another all-out offensive against Kontum. Their engineer units had already been working tirelessly to open new trails to connect their depots in Cambodia to Route 14, as their newly opened Route 70 was already impassable across the high points on the Po Co River. With the weather increasingly dictating tactics, the new attack began on the night of 24 May under cover of an artillery barrage when the 106th and 10th Sapper Battalions began penetrating the southwest sector held by the Regional Forces. They split into small units and sneaked into areas near the airfield, the seminary, and the private residence of the French bishop of Kontum, where they dug in. By early afternoon, after an accurate artillery barrage paralyzed most of the ARVN howitzers, thus forcing their crews to take cover, the new all-out assault was indeed under way. From the north and northwest, infantry and 15 T-54s and T-34-85s swarmed down and penetrated the city, forcing the enemy to give ground, and as night fell the situation became increasingly confused. In the meantime, the two infiltrated sapper battalions threatened to take the vital airfield and by the afternoon the situation was so bleak that a tactical emergency was declared and all available air support was diverted to Kontum, which eventually stabilized the situation.

On 26 May however, the North Vietnamese renewed their assaults against the 53rd Regiment in the northern sector, while pressure also mounted in the south perimeter. The North Vietnamese then made a surprise thrust with two regiments and 20 T-54s and PT-76s against the 44h Regiment held in reserve around the city's hospital complex. Fierce fighting ensued, resulting in a melée between ARVN infantry and PAVN tanks. The UH-1Bs and AH-1Gs swooped down to attack and knocked out six tanks but the North Vietnamese again attacked the 44th Regiment nearly overrunning its defensive positions. Two T-54s came close to the Regimental Command Post firing their guns

directly into the bunker. They were destroyed by ARVN soldiers using their M72 rocket launchers but two other T-54s that were hidden inside ruined houses were destroyed by TOW missiles fired by the gunship helicopters that also knocked out three captured M41s. The enemy penetration was eventually contained by the counter-attack of a battalion of the 44th Regiment, supported by eight M-41s. However, the North Vietnamese infantry still held the northern compound and continued to harass the airfield, forcing US and VNAF supplies to be dropped at a local soccer field. A new penetration by the 45th and 53rd Regiments, supported by 12 tanks, took place that night and the PAVN 64th Regiment concentrated its efforts against the 45th Regiment's positions. Again, diverted B-52 strikes fell on the North Vietnamese, helping to blunt their attack but they could still not be fully thwarted and their dug-in tanks fired directly into ARVN positions. The contested quarters changed hands three times and during these hectic hours the UH-1B detachment played a critical role – firing 21 TOW missiles and knocking out 12 tanks and a truck. The increased artillery shelling did, however, result in the South Vietnamese going without fresh supplies for 24 hours due to the closure of the airfield.

On 27 May, the North Vietnamese again launched another offensive against the northern and southeast perimeters but two T-54s were destroyed inside the ARVN lines by M72s and two others by TOW missiles. By the end of the morning, the South Vietnamese succeeded in stopping their advance, though the North Vietnamese artillery did hit the ARVN main ammunition dump 1km north of the airfield, provoking a series of huge explosions and destroying over 10,000 rounds of artillery munitions – representing 60 percent of all available stock. The VNAF Skyraiders then pressed on and destroyed the anti-aircraft artillery positions the enemy had tried to install around the airfield. Throughout the day the ARVN were supported by 137 tactical sorties flown by the USAF and the VNAF. However, by now, nearly half of the city was in North Vietnamese hands. Consequently, Colonel Ba decided to realign the defense lines and pulled the 53rd Regiment out of FSB November to reinforce the city's perimeter. In the meantime though, the North Vietnamese had seized the field hospital just a block away from the ARVN lines. To the south, the regional forces were now fighting house to house near the school. and a strip of the city next to the airfield where the enemy was hiding. Eventually the North Vietnamese tide began to recede and, as they started to abandon the battlefield, eight more tanks were destroyed.

Over the next four days, 19 C-130 loads were parachuted to a DZ near the city's southwest corner with some 64 tons of munitions delivered, of which the ARVN troops were only able to recover three-quarters. The intensity of the fighting was such that most helicopter supply runs were then suspended. Elsewhere in the northern sector, the communists were also setting a series of pockets that beat off several ARVN counter-attacks supported by tanks. In order to maintain the integrity of his perimeter, Colonel Ba tightened his lines again and on 28 May orders were given to dislodge the North Vietnamese entrenched near the hospital and also on the southern sector – but this was halted due to immediate enemy machine gun fire that was only eventually silenced by a TOW-armed UH-1B. Throughout the day, the North Vietnamese were gradually pushed back and expelled, losing two additional T-54s – and despite continuing bad weather the VNAF A-37s and Cobra helicopters passed underneath the cloud bases to attack the forward 14th Armored Cavalry Squadron that had fallen into enemy hands. The 53rd Regiment was thus able to cross the area safely before attacking 500m into the airfield where the regiment fought hand-to-hand with the enemy until early evening. On the afternoon of 28 May, Kontum was reinforced by the 3rd Battalion of the 47th Regiment of the 22nd Division from Pleiku.

The next day, 60 tactical air support sorties targeted suspected artillery positions but the PAVN were not going to be easily defeated. Again they attacked the northeast sector that same night and their heroism stunned both the South Vietnamese and their American advisors. The bunker-to-bunker advance continued until 30 May when the ARVN had retaken most of the lost territory inside Kontum. With the steadying of the situation and with the easier food and ammunition drops, President Thieu flew into the city on the afternoon of 30 May and pinned the Brigadier General Star on Colonel Ba in a very rare battlefield promotion. The next day the battle was declared over by Saigon, even if there were still a couple of resistance pockets that would take until the following week to be fully overcome. However, with over 4,000 dead PAVN soldiers and dozens of tanks littering the battlefield that evening, the human cost had been very high.

With this, the 320A Division withdrew towards Tan Canh while the 2nd Division returned to its jungle redoubt in Quang Ngai Province. They were constantly targeted by air attacks during their withdrawal with the B-52s attacking 145 regrouping and refitting areas between 6–30 June. Upon Director Vann's request, the USAF C-130 landings resumed on the night of 8–9 June when six Hercules made blacked-out radar-controlled approaches and landings whilst friendly artillery fire was directed into any likely danger area to discourage enemy shelling, and flare shells were detonated near the runway in the hope of distracting any SAM-7 missiles. Throughout the campaign in the Central Highlands air-power played a critical role in blunting the

North Vietnamese offensive, with the B-52 bombers flying 874 sorties during four months of battle, which certainly helped the ARVN both tactically and psychologically by raising morale. Despite the obvious brute force of carpet-bombing, the fighting also drew in a new era of precision-guided munitions with the deployment of new systems like the TOW. The small Aerial TOW Team, deployed in only two UH-1B helicopters, fired 162 missiles in combat – of which 151 worked – and 124 hit their targets. The unit claimed 11 T-54s, seven PT-76s, seven M41s, three M113s, six trucks and three artillery pieces. The American advisors also closely monitored the performance of the VNAF in the II Corps and USAF senior advisor, Colonel Van Brussel, was very heartened by the overall performance of the South Vietnamese pilots – particularly those flying the A-37s. Sortie-for-sortie, the A-37 crews destroyed more communist tanks than the Americans – in part reflecting the stability and turning capability of the A-37 and its ability to operate under adverse weather – and one VNAF pilot was even recognized for destroying five enemy tanks and damaging several others at Kontum. The FAC observation units also worked well handling the VNAF and American fighter bombers, whilst the helicopter and transport squadrons fulfilled their duties well. However, the VNAF units, equipped with less advanced aircraft, paid a heavy price against enemy flak and the 530th Fighter Squadron based at Pleiku lost nine of its Skyraiders – which would certainly have worried the ARVN considering that America would soon be withdrawing its air support from the country.

By 30 June, the last PAVN blocking forces around Kontum were eliminated and truck convoys could now reach the city but, due to the limited reserve of ARVN assets, the South Vietnamese could not actually travel more than 10km northwest of Kontum when the ceasefire came into effect. In the southeast, the refitted 22nd Division retook the Hoai Thon and Tam Quang Districts at the end of the summer and reopened Route 1 to traffic. Sadly, the man who contributed so much to the ARVN success in MR II, Director Vann, did not live long enough to savor the victory because he died when his helicopter crashed on 9 June during a night flight between Pleiku and Kontum. He was succeeded by Brigadier General Michael Healy who was a former Special Forces officer. When the ceasefire came into effect in January 1973, the South Vietnamese still controlled most of the Central Highlands but their forces retained only a precarious hold on the northwestern sector. More worrisome, they had been pushed back from all the outposts along the Laotian border that overlooked the Ho Chi Minh Trail and it was felt that it would only be a matter of time before the PAVN would recover and attack again, yet this actual last offensive against the South Vietnamese would take three years to develop, starting from the Central Highlands once again.

CHAPTER 8
AFTERMATH

By the fall, the North and South Vietnamese were exhausted, with neither side having enough resources to break the stalemate and both waiting to see what would happen at the new peace talks. Thus, the ARVN was unable to reclaim all lost territories whilst the PAVN was focused on consolidating its rural 'liberated' areas, roughly a buffer zone along the borders to strengthen its logistical system. The communists had also tried in vain to derail the South Vietnamese

pacification programs in other parts of South Vietnam, particularly in the Mekong Delta, where they infiltrated several regiments and battalions but were quickly defeated. The PAVN 1st Division tried to add its weight to the battle but the South Vietnamese beat this move too by attacking its bases in Cambodia. Even elements of the 5th and 9th Divisions that attacked the Kien Tuong Province in the northwest of the Mekong Delta Area were quickly pushed back by the

A technician from a Hughes Aircraft climbs over a destroyed T-54B to inspect it after being hit by a TOW missile. It was one of 10 T-54s claimed by the NUH-1B gunship helicopters. (Hughes Aircraft)

ARVN 7th Division. The South Vietnamese themselves made small incursions into Cambodia and retook the town of Kompong Trabek but neither side made big attempts nor took risky actions. Then, on the eve of the US presidential election, Henry Kissinger and the North Vietnamese Politburo member Le Duc Tho met in Paris, and the stalemate melted. Tho presented a North Vietnamese plan which included proposals for a ceasefire; the withdrawal of American forces; an exchange of prisoners of war, whilst Hanoi no longer demanded that President Thieu be removed from office; and the Americans could continue its aid of the South. However, the South Vietnamese rejected the proposed scheme (drafted without their input) because none of their demands had been met, such as the withdrawal of all foreign forces including those of North Vietnam, and the recognition of the 17th Parallel as an international boundary. President Nixon tried to negotiate with both sides but failed, and subsequently the United States launched Operation Linebacker II against the North. This unprecedented air offensive began on 18 December in Hanoi and Haiphong with B-52 bombers and lasted 12 days (with a truce for Christmas) with the massive planes flying 795 sorties and dropping 15,237 tons of bombs. In addition, 769 tactical sorties were flown by the USAF and 505 sorties by the US Navy and the USMC; meaning an additional 5,000 tons of bombs was dropped. In total, about around 15 B-52s were brought down and nine damaged whilst 12 tactical aircraft were also lost. North Vietnam's infrastructure was badly smashed. However, with over 500 rail interdictions, an estimated three million gallons of petroleum was destroyed and 80 percent of North Vietnam's electrical power zapped.

However, even with this Operation, it wasn't until 27 January 1973 that the Peace Accord was finally signed in Paris – an agreement that looked a lot like the one presented by North Vietnam in October. The demanded withdrawal of the PAVN units from South Vietnam was not mentioned at all but Henry Kissinger did manage to get a 'verbal agreement' for the withdrawal of 30,000 North Vietnamese troops, with Washington then agreeing to pay war reparations to Hanoi. The North Vietnamese leadership rightly considered the agreement a great victory even if they had lost 100,000 men, versus some 44,000 South Vietnamese and 198 Americans. The PAVN had also lost nearly half of its artillery and two-thirds of its tanks, with over 450 armored vehicles destroyed. From a tactical perspective then, the Nguyen Hue Offensive had been a failure and thus their first venture into conventional mechanized operations had major shortcomings. Even so, the offensive was launched by General Giap in haste with the firm belief that he had no choice in order to grab the 'strategic upper hand' in forcing Washington to quit Vietnam. This model is known as the 'Dau Tranh', or 'one struggle concept' that integrates military, political ideological, economic and diplomatic efforts. The whole nation was mobilized for the war and every citizen a 'fighter' becoming mere 'tools of war'. With this, final victory would not be reached by a decisive battle but by a series of campaigns with a strategy to wear down its enemies both militarily and politically, to undermine its economy and its will to further the conflict. Yet these were sacrifices that Hanoi's leadership were willing to endure in their crusade to expel any 'foreign invaders' from the country. Facing this, the Saigon regime could not present a united front because they were mired by factionalism and corruption but, as during the 1968 Tet Offensive, the ARVN had not collapsed under its deficiencies, but fought back heroically. The United States entered the Vietnam War with only limited strategic aims within the wider context of the Cold War, mostly the 'containment' of Red China, and confident that their military superiority could achieve victory quickly. They were not prepared for a protracted war and facing growing political, economical and societal problems at home; they just wanted to leave Southeast Asia with as few casualties as possible.

The already weakened position of General Giap within the Politburo since the death in 1969 of his mentor, Chairman Ho Chi Minh, was further exacerbated by the heavy losses suffered on the battlefield. He was replaced as commander of the PAVN by his

The commander of the ARVN 23rd Division, Colonel Ly Tong Ba (center), poses with his senior advisor, Colonel Rhotenberry (left), beside a captured North Vietnamese T-54 tank during the closing stages of the Kontum battle. (US Army)

loyal deputy, General Van Tien Dung. However, Giap retained the post of Defence Minister and continued to exercise considerable influence by continuing to direct the Central Military Commission. The North Vietnamese Army themselves would learn and assimilate the lessons of the failed offensive, devoting great effort to continuing and improving its performances in mechanized operations. Many ARVN shortcomings, particularly the reshuffling of its inadequate High Command structures, had been made under duress of war and the structure of South Vietnam made these changes difficult. Some sources even suggest that President Nixon warned President Thieu he faced being overthrown and that aid would be cut if he continued to object to the terms of the peace agreement. However, the situation was softened in a series of personal letters where President Nixon promised the return of B-52s should the North Vietnamese significantly 'violate the accord'.

As the peace process developed, it is indeed apparent that the Americans clearly favored the communist side, wanting a clean and quick 'getaway' from the country, a total American withdrawal and the release of the US and South Vietnamese prisoners. The agreement allowed the North Vietnamese to maintain their troops in their 'occupied' areas of the South. Thus, the future of South Vietnam now relied on a 'permanent ceasefire' to be monitored by an international neutral team of 1,160 observers. A National Council of Reconciliation and Concord would also be set up to organize future elections in South Vietnam. However, that body was to operate on the basis of unanimity, which under the circumstances was a formula for paralysis. Indeed, with the peace agreement, Washington had just bought what Henry Kissinger called a 'decent interval' for the United States to disengage from the area. Yet in finalizing the Peace Accord the way they did, the days of South Vietnam were numbered because two-and-a-half years later after recovering from the huge losses of the Easter Offensive, Hanoi launched the ultimate campaign against a now abandoned South Vietnam.

Bibliography

Andrade, Dale, *America's Last Vietnam Battle; Halting Hanoi's 1972 Easter Offensive* (Lawrence KS: University Press of Kansas, 2001).

Ang Cheng Guan, *The Vietnam War from the Other Side: The Vietnamese Communists' Perspective* (London & New York: Routledge Curzon (Taylor & Francis), 2002).

Bowers, Ray L., *Tactical Airlift* (Washington: Office of Air Force History & GPO, 1983).

Brigham, Robert K., *ARVN: Life and Death in the South Vietnamese Army* (Lawrence KS: University Press of Kansas, 2006).

Des Brisay, Captain Thomas D., *Fourteen Hours at Koh Tang. USAF Southeast Asia Monograph Series. Volume III, Monographs 4 & 5* (Washington DC: GPO, 1977).

Cao Van Vien, General, & Dong Van Khuyen, Lietenant General, *Indochina Monographs: Reflections on the Vietnam War* (Washington DC: GPO, 1980).

Cao Van Vien, General, & Ngo Quang Truong, Lieutenant General, & Dong Van Khuyen, Lieutenant General, & Nguyen Duy Hinh, Major General, & Tran Dinh Tho, Colonel Brigadier General, & Hoang Ngoc Lung, & Chu Xuan Vien, Lietenat Colonel, *Indochina Monographs: The U.S. Adviser* (Washington DC: GPO, 1980).

Cao Van Vien, General, *Indochina Monographs: Leadership* (Washington DC: GPO, 1980).

Clodfelter, Mark, *The Limits of Air Power: The American Bombing of North Vietnam* (New York: The Free Press, 1989).

Collins Jr., Brigadier General James, *The Development and Training of the South Vietnamese Army, 1950-1972* (Washington DC: Department of the Army, 1986).

Conboy, Ken, & Bowra, Ken, *The NVA and Viet Cong* (Oxford: Osprey Publishing, 1991).

Conboy, Ken, *Shadow War; the CIA's Secret War in Laos* (Boulder CO: Paladin Press, 1995).

Cosmos, Graham A., & Murray, Terrence P, *U.S. Marines in Vietnam: Vietnamization and Redeployment, 1970-1971* (Washington DC: History & Museums Division, 1986).

Da Nguyen Xuan Mau, *Dien Bien Phu Tren Khong: Hoi Ky / Dien Bien Phu Battle of the Sky 1972* (Hanoi: Nha Xuat Ban Chinh Tri Quoc Gia, 2007).

Despuech, Jacques C., *L'offensive du Vendredi Saint* (Paris: Fayard, 1973).

Doglione, Colonel John A., *Airpower and the 1972 Spring Invasion. USAF Southeast Asia Monograph Series Volume II* (Washington DC: GPO, 1976).

Dong Van Khuyen, Lietenant General, *Indochina Monographs: RVNAF Logistics* (Washington DC: GPO, 1980).

Dorr, Robert F., *Air War South Vietnam* (London: Arms & Armour Press, 1990).

Duiker, William J., *Sacred War: Nationalism and Revolution in a Divided Vietnam* (New York: McGraw-Hill, 1995).

Grandolini, Albert, *Armor of the Vietnam War; Asian Forces* (Hong Kong: Concord Publications Company, 1998).

Ha Mai Viet, *Steel and Blood: South Vietnamese Armor and the War for Southeast Asia.* (Annapolis MD: Naval Institute Press, 2008).

Jackson, George J., *Linebacker II: An Examination of Strategic Use of Air Power* (Maxwell AFB, AL: Air University, 1989).

Lam Quang Thi, *The Twenty-Five Year Century: A South Vietnamese General Remembers the Indochina War to the Fall of Saigon* (Denton TX: University of North Texas Press, 2001).

Lam Quang Thi, *Hell in An Loc. The 1972 Easter Invasion and the Battle that Saved South Vietnam* (Denton TX: University of North Texas Press, 2009).

Larsen, Lietenant General Stanley R., & Collins, Brigadier General James L Jr., *Allied Participation in Vietnam* (Washington DC: GPO, 1975).

Le Hai Trieu, *Su doan 10: binh doan Tay nguyen* (Hanoi: Nha xuat Ban Quan Doi Nhan Dan / Vietnam People's Army Publishing House, 1987).

Lien-Hang T. Nguyen, *Hanoi's War: An International History of the War for Peace in Vietnam* (Chapel Hill NC: University of North Carolina Press, 2012).

McCarthy, Brigader General James R. & Rayfield, Colonel Robert E., *Linebacker II: A View from the Rock. USAF Southeast Asia Monograph Series. Volume VI,* (Maxwell AFB, AL: Air War College, 1979).

McKenna, Thomas P., *Kontum, the battle to save South Vietnam* (Lexington KY: The University Press of Kentucky, 2011).

Melson, Charles D., & Curtis, Arnold G., *U.S. Marines in Vietnam: The War that Would Not End, 1971-1973* (Washington DC: History & Museums Division, 1991).

Melson, Charles D., & Hannon, Paul, *Vietnam Marines 1965-1973* (Oxford: Osprey Publishing Ltd, 2012).

Mesko, Jim, *VNAF: South Vietnamese Air Force: 1945-1975* (Carrollton TX: Squadron/Signal Publications, 1987).

Mikesh, Robert C., *Flying Dragons: The South Vietnamese Air Force* (London: Osprey Publishing, 1988).

Miller, Grider, John, *The Bridge at Dong Ha.* (Annapolis MD: Naval Institute Press, 1989).

Momyer, General William, *The Vietnamese Air Force, 1951-1975, an Analysis of its Role in Combat. USAF Southeast Asia Monograph Series. Volume III, Monographs 4 & 5* (Washington DC: GPO, 1977)

Nalty, Bernard C., *Air War over South Vietnam, 1968-1975* (Washington DC: Air Force History & Museums Program, 2001).

Ngo Quang Truong, Lieutenant General, *Indochina Monographs: The Easter Offensive of 1972* (Washington DC: GPO, 1979).

Ngo Quang Truong, Lieutenant General, *Indochina Monographs: RVNAF and US Operational Cooperation and Coordination* (Washington DC: GPO, 1980).

Ngo Quang Truong, Lieutenant General, *Indochina Monographs: Territorial Forces.* (Washington DC: GPO, 1980).

Nguyen Duc Phuong, *Chien Thanh Viet Nam, Toan Tap, Tu Tran Dau (Ap Bac–1963) den Tran Cuoi (Saigon-1975). The Vietnam War, from the first (Ap Bac–1963) to the last (Saigon-1975) battles* (Toronto: Lang Van Publishers, 2001).

Nguyen Duy Hinh, Major General, & Tran Dinh Tho, Brigadier General, *Indochina Monographs: The South Vietnamese Society* (Washington DC: GPO, 1980).

Nguyen Duy Hinh, Major General, *Indochina Monographs: Vietnamization and the Cease-Fire* (Washington DC: GPO, 1980).

Nguyen Manh Dan, & Nguyen Ngoc Hanh, *Vietnam in flames. The General Staff of the Armed Forces of the Republic of Vietnam* (Saigon, 1971).

Pham Phong Dinh, *Chien Su Quan Luc Viet Nam Cong Hoa.* (Winnipeg: Tu Sach Vinh Danh, 2001). One chapter for each division, and each other major component of the RVNAF, in the 1970s.

Prados, John, *Vietnam: The History of an Unwinnable War, 1945-1975* (Lawrence KS: University Press of Kansas, 2009)

Pribbenow, Merle L.; Military History Institute of Vietnam. *Victory in Vietnam: The Official History of the People's Army of Vietnam 1954 -1975* (Lawrence KS: University of Kansas Press, 2002).

Randolph, Stephan P., *Powerful and Brutal Weapons: Nixon, Kissinger, and the Easter Offensive* (London: Harvard University Press, 2007).

Rottman, Gordon L., *Khe Sanh 1967–1968; Marines battle for Vietnam's vital hilltop base. Campaign Series* (Oxford: Osprey Publishing, 2005).

Rottman, Gordon L. & Bujeiro, Ramiro, *Army of the Republic of Vietnam 1955–75* (Oxford: Osprey Publishing, 2010).

Rottman, Gordon L. & Volstad, Ron, *Vietnam Airborne* (Oxford: Osprey Publishing, 2012).

Sheehan, Neil, *A Bright Shining Lie* (London: Pimlico Edition, 1998).

Smith, John T., *The Linebacker Raids: The bombing of North Vietnam, 1972* (London: Arms & Armour Press, 1998).

Starry, General Don A., *Vietnam Studies Series: Mounted Combat in Vietnam.* (Washington DC: US Army Center of Military History 1977).

Stockwell, David B., *Tanks in the Wire! The first use of enemy armor in Vietnam* (New York: Penguin, 1990).

Thompson, Wayne, *To Hanoi and Back: The U.S. Air Force and North Vietnam, 1966-1973* (Washington DC: Smithsonian Institution Press, 2000).

Tilford, Jr. Earl H., *Set up: What the Air Force Did in Vietnam and Why* (Maxwell AFB AL: Air University Press, 1991).

Tran Dinh Tho, Brigadier General, *Indochina Monographs: The Cambodian Incursion* (Washington DC: GPO 1979).

Tran Dinh Tho, Brigadier General, *Indochina Monographs: Pacification* (Washington DC: GPO, 1980).

Tran Van Tra, *Nhung chang duong lich su cu B2 thanh dong*, 5 vols projected. Vol. 5, *Ket thuc cuoc chien tranh 30 nam*, was published first, (Ho Chi Minh City: Van Nghe, 1982), and was translated as *Vietnam: History of the Bulwark B-2 Theatre Volume 5: Concluding the 30-Years War*, JPRS 82783 (Springfield, VA: NTIS, 1983). It covered the period from 1973 to 1975.

Tran Xuan Dung, ed., *History of the Vietnamese Marine Corps, Army of the Republic of Vietnam/Chien Su Thuy Quan Luc Chien, Quan Luc Viet Nam Cong Hoa* (Toronto, 1997).

US Army Center of Military History, *Vietnam Studies Series: Nguyen Duy Hinh. Lam Son 719* (Washington DC: US Army CMH, 1979).

Vietnamese Military History Institute, *Su Doan Quan Tien Phong – Su Doan 308 / 308th Division History* (Hanoi: Nha Xuat Ban Quan Doi Nhan Dan / Vietnam People's Army Publishing House, 1979).

Vietnamese Military History Institute, *Lich Su Binh Chung Thiet Giap Quan Doi Nhan Dan Viet Nam 1959–1975 / Armour Corps History 1959–1979* (Hanoi: Nha Xuat Ban Quan Doi Nhan Dan / Vietnam People's Army Publishing House, 1982).

Vietnamese Military History Institute, *Su doan Sao Vang: Binh doan Chi Lang Quan khu 1 / The Gold Star Division: Chi Lang Corps, Military Region 1* (Hanoi: NXB Quan Doi Nhan Dan / Vietnam People's Army Publishing House, 1984).

Vietnamese Military History Institute, *Su Doan 303 / 303rd Division History* (Hanoi: Nha Xuat Ban Quan Doi Nhan Dan / Vietnam People's Army Publishing House, 1989).

Vietnamese Military History Institute, *Lich Su Lu Doan Tang 203 / 203rd Armoured Brigade History* (Hanoi: Quan Doan 2 Xuat Ban / Vietnam People's Army Publishing House, 1990).

Vietnamese Military History Institute, *Su Doan 7 / 7th Division History* (Hanoi: Nha Xuat Ban Quan Doi Nhan Dan / Vietnam People's Army Publishing House, 1990).

Vietnamese Military History Institute, *Lich Su Cong Binh Viet Nam 1945–1975 / Engineer Corps History 1945–1975* (Hanoi: Nha Xuat Ban Quan Doi Nhan Dan / Vietnam People's Army Publishing House, 1991).

Vietnamese Military History Institute, *Lich Su Quan Chung Phong Khong. 2 vols. / PAVN Air defense units in both of the Indochina wars* (Hanoi: Nha Xuat Ban Quan Doi Nhan / Vietnam People's Army Publishing House, 1991 & 1993).

Vietnamese Military History Institute, *Tu Dien Bach Khoa Quan Su Viet Nam. Bo Quoc Phong. / Vietnamese Military Dictionary* (Hanoi: Nha Xuat Ban Quan Doi Nhan Dan / Vietnam People's Army Publishing House, 1996).

Whitcomb, Darrel D., *The Rescue of Bat 21* (Annapolis MD: Naval Institute Press, 1998).

Wiest, Andrew, *Vietnam's Forgotten Army: Heroism and Betrayal in the ARVN* (New York: NYU Press, 2008).

Willbanks, James H., *The Battle of An Loc* (Bloomington IND: Indiana University Press, 2005).

Acknowledgments

The author wishes to express his gratitude to all those who contributed to this book. Specifically, I wish to express my deepest appreciation to Anthony J. Tambini, Cao Tan Loc, Chau Huu Loc, Dang Huy Lang, Do Khac Mai, Ha Minh Tay, Ho Dac Du, Ha Mai Viet, Huynh Sanh Thong, Huynh Ba Phuc, Huynh Thu Thoai, Jean Dunoyer, Jean Pierre Hoehn, Ken Conboy, Le Quang Thuan, Le Xuan Lan, Mai Van Hai, Nguyen Tien Van, Nguyen Xuan Giac, Pham Long Suu, Pham Quang Khiem, Robert C. Mikesk, Roger Routin, Stephane Legoff, Ted Koppel, Terry Love, Timothy Keer, Timothy Pham, Tom Cooper, Tran Tan Tiep, Ung Buu Hoang Nguyen, Victor Flintham, Vo Ngoc Cac, Vu Dinh and to all the other people who wish to stay anonymous, fearing for the safety of their families.

Everybody in some way or another helped me with the research and made this book possible.

Albert Grandolini

Military historian and aviation-journalist, Albert Grandolini, was born in France and gained an MA in history from Paris I Sorbonne University. His primary research focus is on contemporary conflicts in general and particularly on the military history of Asia. Having spent his childhood in South Vietnam, the Vietnam War has been one of his main fields of research. He is the author of the books *The Fall of the Flying Dragon, South Vietnamese Air Force (1973-1975)* with Harpia Publishing and *Armor of the Vietnam War: the Asian Forces*, Concord Publishing. He is also co-author of the two volumes on Libyan Air Wars with Helion in the *Africa@War* Series. He has also written numerous articles for various British, French and German magazines such as *Air Enthusiast, Flieger Revue Extra, Fana de l'aviation, Tank Zone* and *Batailles et Blindés*. He has regularly contributed to the Air Combat Information Group (ACIG) and the *Au Delà de la Colline* military history French website.